Heroes
and Villains
of New Mexico

HEROES
and VILLAINS
of NEW MEXICO

A Collection of True Stories

Bud Russo

SUNSTONE
PRESS

SANTA FE

Sunstone books may be purchased for educational, business, or sales promotional use. For information please write: Special Markets Department, Sunstone Press, P.O. Box 2321, Santa Fe, New Mexico 87504-2321.

Book and cover design › Vicki Ahl
Body typeface › Book Antiqua
Printed on acid-free paper
∞
eBook 978-1-61139-552-5

Library of Congress Cataloging-in-Publication Data

Names: Russo, Bud, 1943- author.
Title: Heroes and villains of New Mexico : a collection of true stories / by
 Bud Russo.
Description: Santa Fe : Sunstone Press, [2018] | Includes bibliographical
 references.
Identifiers: LCCN 2018011158 (print) | LCCN 2018022480 (ebook) | ISBN
 9781611395525 | ISBN 9781632932259 (softcover : alk. paper)
Subjects: LCSH: New Mexico--Biography. | Heroes--New Mexico--Biography. | New
 Mexico--History--Anecdotes.
Classification: LCC F795 (ebook) | LCC F795 .R87 2018 (print) | DDC
 978.9--dc23
LC record available at https://lccn.loc.gov/2018011158

WWW.SUNSTONEPRESS.COM
SUNSTONE PRESS / POST OFFICE BOX 2321 / SANTA FE, NM 87504-2321 /USA
(505) 988-4418 / ORDERS ONLY (800) 243-5644 / FAX (505) 988-1025

To my Huckleberry Friend

Wherever you are
We are always together.

Contents

Preface

There's an old saying: "Life is stranger than fiction." As I have traveled New Mexico, writing stories for radio, local newspapers, and magazines about the people, places, history, and culture of the Land of Enchantment, I've come across tales that make me chuckle. I think, *This just can't be true.* Yet when I delve into the story and do a bit of research, I find indeed the old adage is unquestionably correct. I have been led to stories of "real" people living in "real" times, whose adventures indeed *are* stranger than fiction.

Some stories have legends associated with them. Billy the Kid readily comes to mind. To be completely transparent and not disappoint you, Billy does not appear in this book, except by circumstance—when he encountered other people, whose stories are here. There have been just too many books and films about Billy, and half of what you read or see is legend; at least, there is little irrefutable, empirical evidence to substantiate the tales associated with his twenty-two year-long life. Other tales incorporate ghosts or strange apparitions. The stories in this collection don't need to be enhanced by fanciful imagination. They are real. The events happened just as I have presented them. They are about people who lived in New Mexico from when Don Juan de Oñate trekked north from Mexico City until the mid-twentieth century.

I've tried to select stories that bridge cultures—from Puebloan and Native American, to Spanish, to Anglo—linking the histories of aboriginal America, Spain, Mexico, and the United States. These stories are about individuals, people who accomplished much or got into serious trouble. Some died for their troubles. Some survived despite adversity. Some simply flourished. But their stories are not just about them. They are about moments in history that have defined New Mexico. They speak to the spirit of the people, their fortitude and determination, their kindness and humanity, their vision of what they could accomplish. They also speak of the greed, cruelty, and indifference of some people—characteristics undoubtedly contributing to Congress' denial fourteen times of New Mexico Territory's petition for statehood over a period of more than sixty years.

As you read through this collection, you will have to determine who were heroes and who were villains. Some are obvious. Sally Rooke is unquestionably a heroine. Black Jack Ketchum, on the other hand, is undeniably a villain. Some could be either hero or villain and, from extenuating circumstances in their lives, some could be both—at one time, hero; at other times, villain. Kit Carson, seen from the vantage of Anglos, who watched him try to save Ann White, would consider him hero. Navajo readers, whose ancestors were victims of Carson's scorched-earth practice to round up the Dinè and march them on The Long Walk to the horror that was Bosque Redondo, might see him as villain. In the end, you will have to decide for yourself who is hero and who is villain.

These stories are about people whose names you may recognize. The events of their lives are part of authentic history, skillfully researched and presented by many well-known historians and biographers. But you may never before have encountered these particular episodes of their lives. None of the stories is overly long. You can read one in a few minutes. And, when you have finished them, I hope you will have been entertained and informed, learning something you didn't know before, something that both enriches your sense of our humanity and your understanding of what is so enchanting about New Mexico.

I have included bibliographical references for further reading, should your curiosity encourage you to delve deeper into the lives of one or more of these New Mexicans.

Spanish Colonial Period

1598-1820

Pedro de Peralta — Governor
He battled a friar for dominion.

In the 17th century, Spanish governors of the Province of Nuevo México were constantly at odds with church leaders. Governors paid the king for the privilege of being governor and then had to raise enough money to reclaim the king's ransom as well as whatever wealth they needed to live the good life afterwards.

Franciscan friars saw their mission as first converting the heathen to Christianity and then protecting them from the predatory practices of the governor. But...and this is an important point...friars demanded the people build lavish churches and *conventos* — or residences — for them, raise food and livestock for them, and contribute money for their welfare and upkeep.

The tug-of-war was constant and usually nobody won, especially people caught between the Spanish governor and the Spanish friars.

In 1609, Luis de Velasco, *marqués de Salinas* and viceroy of Mexico, appointed Pedro de Peralta to the post of governor and the latest round in the war between church and state began.

Peralta replaced Juan de Oñate, the first governor who had head-quartered the colony at the pueblo of Ohkay Owingeh in 1598, renaming it San Juan in honor of his patron saint. The new governor relocated the capital a few miles south, naming it *La Villa Real de la Santa Fe de San Francisco de Asís* — The Royal Town of the Holy Faith of St. Francis of Assisi. Today, we simply call the city Santa Fe.

The new governor selected a site along the Rió Santa Fe with ample land and adequate water. His surveyors laid out the town, including a plaza around which were government offices, a jail, arsenal, and a chapel. The governor's headquarters was a palace built for defense with three-foot-thick adobe walls. The Palace of the Governors is the oldest continuously occupied building in the United States and, for nearly two decades, it has housed the Museum of New Mexico.

Franciscans assumed their main objective in New Mexico was to convert Indians. They argued they had a duty to protect the Indians from abuses by the military and civilians, and they believed civil power existed only for protection and support this goal.

The governor, as chief magistrate and head of the army, had different ideas about the use of power. To weaken the church's position, Peralta issued strict regulations imposing imprisonment of ten days by civil authority for any Spaniard, including priests, found guilty of abusing an Indian worker. There was plenty of abuse to go around. Perhaps from cleverness or for revenge, Indians deliberately provoked violence to earn the fine.

Clashes were inevitable.

A wagon train arrived in Santa Fe in 1612, bringing Fray Isidro de Ordóñez to the colony. He had been in New Mexico twice previously and, this time, came as the leader of the nine Franciscan friars in residence. He also claimed to be the Inquisitor General for the Spanish Inquisition in New Mexico. When he reached Nuestra Señora de los Dolores, the southernmost mission at Sandia Pueblo, Ordóñez produced a document purportedly naming him Father Commissary, or head of the New Mexican church. When the documents were presented to the governor, Peralta flatly refused to accept them or acknowledge the priest's authority, claiming the documents were forged.

In Santa Fe, Ordóñez sought to redeem his dominance and power. He proclaimed any soldier or colonist could leave, if he so chose, a proclamation undermining Peralta's authority. The governor's response was to stifle the friar's activities. Meanwhile, Ordóñez accused the governor of denying food to Indians engaged in the construction of Santa Fe.

The battle was joined. The struggle for who would control the colony intensified.

To get the upper hand, Ordóñez accused Peralta of being a schismatic heretic and excommunicated him in May 1613, posting the announcement on the doors of the church. He ordered the governor arrested, shackled in chains, and imprisoned at the Sandia mission. Fray Esteban de Perea, in charge of the jail, disapproved but, with a sense of self-preservation, he obeyed. From the pulpit, with crucifix in hand, Ordóñez broadcast his desire to be named bishop for the righteous act of imprisoning the unrepentant and unyielding governor.

Ordóñez was now in total control of the colony, wielding both civil and religious power. As head of the Inquisition, the friar had the authority to excommunicate, even if the charges were bogus and his motives self-serving. Who, if any, would challenge him?

Peralta was incarcerated for nearly a year, although he did escape for a brief time, walking in winter, half naked and wrapped in a buffalo robe, to a ranch five miles away, where he was able to dispatch a message to the viceroy in Mexico City. He was recaptured and remained imprisoned until Bernardino de Ceballos, the new temporal governor, arrived in the spring of 1614. Even then, the deposed governor was not allowed to leave until fall, giving the friar and new governor time to abscond with Peralta's possessions.

Shipped to Mexico City in chains, Peralta appealed to the viceroy and Mexican Inquisition. He told his version of the dispute with Ordóñez and was vindicated. The Mexican Inquisitor General eventually ordered Ordóñez back to Mexico City, where he was reprimanded.

Shortly after his vindication, Peralta was appointed *alcalde mayor* of the port of Acapulco. Then, he moved to Caracas, in what is now Venezuela, where he served as an official in the royal treasury in the 1640s and early 1650s. He later resigned this commission and returned to Madrid, where he lived in retirement until his death in 1666.

Now, you'd think this story would end here, but the name, Peralta, lived on for nearly two centuries.

In the late 1800s, James Reavis popularized the idea of a rich Peralta family who had lived and ruled over part of the American Southwest. He contended there was a land grant and barony granted by the King of Spain to Peralta. It included Superstition Mountains, purportedly the site of the Lost Dutchman's Gold Mine. Dr. George M. Willing, a territorial delegate to Congress, claimed to have purchased the land grant from a man named Miguel Peralta. Reavis became Willing's partner in defending the claim and initially the U.S. government indicated their documents supported the legitimacy of the land grant.

Meanwhile, Reavis married a woman he claimed was the Peralta heiress to the barony of Arizona and assumed the title of baron. He duped some people in the disputed land grant to pay him for quitclaims on their existing properties and sold other property to investors. Reavis was exposed for forging Peralta genealogy and other documents and served a prison sentence for fraud. Dr. Willing, his partner, escaped punishment. Death had claimed him in 1874.

Diego Romero—Captain of the Apache Nation
His little head did the thinking for his big head

There really is truth in the statement: the little head did the thinking for the big head. The dictionary defines the phrase as "The inability of the human male to process information clearly; attributed to a sudden, overwhelming hormonal influx produced by non-physical sexual stimuli."

In the case of *Sargento Major* Diego Romero, clear thinking with his big head might have saved his life. But, I am getting ahead of my story.

Romero was caught up in a power struggle between Fray Alonso de Posada, *custos* or agent of the Inquisition, and Don Bernardo López de Mendizábal, governor of the Province of Nuevo México. Such power struggles existed in Spanish Colonial New Mexico every since Don Juan de Oñate traveled north from Mexico City in 1598 with his contingent of colonists and, undoubtedly, priests.

Governors paid the king of Spain for the privilege of being governor, then had to recover their investment and whatever other wealth they coveted during their tenure. That generally meant they virtually—if not actually—enslaved the local people to produce food, hides, and other valuables the governor could sell in Mexico City, there being no gold found by the Spanish in the province. Meanwhile, the church took upon itself the task of protecting people they were trying to Christianize, although they levied hardships nearly as heavy as those of the government. The local populace was required to build a church—not a chapel, but an edifice rivaling any in Spain—plus the *convento* or priests' residence, stables, corrals, and other buildings, as well as provide food for the priests and labor for all the lay positions.

In May 1661, *Custos* Posada began hearing charges against the governor for dismissing *alcaldes* or mayors and confiscating their *encomiendas* or tribute due from the Puebloans. By the time Posada was ready to act on charges, López de Mendizábal had been replaced by Don Diego de Peñalosa Briceño. Only the name had changed. One governor after another put the "squeeze" on subordinates.

The Holy Office in Mexico City had already ordered the arrest of López de Mendizábal and three of his co-conspirators. Among them was *Sargento Mayor* Diego Romero, former *alcalde ordinario* or municipal magistrate of Santa Fe. Thus, the Inquisition moved against the men.

John Kessell, in his book, *Kiva, Cross & Crown,* writes, "Up to that time the Holy Office made its sudden arrests, New Mexico had seemed big enough for both *Custos* Posada and Governor Peñalosa. They had even cooperated." However, Posada ordered *alcalde majores* to impound *encomienda,* an act infuriating the governor. Peñalosa challenged the friar's orders, and Posada responded by embargoing all property belonging to the prisoners. In short, the church claimed the wealth flowing into the coffers of the governor.

Among the four prisoners, whom the Inquisition had condemned as apostates and heretics, was Diego Romero. During his trial, he implicated his fellow prisoners and admitted he was a crude and ignorant man. Besides confiscation of material goods, Romero had been accused of incest with Juana Romero, allegedly his cousin and mother of his son. He swore she was no relative but a *mestiza* his mother had raised from infancy. The blond-haired child, he said, was not his but the son of Juana from the Father Guardian of the Santa Fe *convento.*

It is conceivable, Romero's story would have ended here, with the loss of the expropriated goods and sufficient proof he had not acted incestuously with his cousin.

However, other charges, stemming from an unusual circumstance among the Apaches living on the plains to the east, were brought against him.

Sergeant Romero had been sent by López de Mendizábal on a

trading mission, along with *El Carpentiero*, a leader of the Cicuye Pueblo (known by Anglos as Pecos Pueblo). Romero so befriended the Apaches, they chose to appoint him as *capitán grande de toda la Nación apache* – chief captain of the entire Apache nation.

One afternoon, some 30 braves appeared in Romero's camp and circled around him. Four of them picked up the heavy-set Romero and laid him on a buffalo hide. Then, they hoisted him shoulder high and carried them in procession, performing a ritual accompanied by singing and reed flutes. They bore him to their *rancheria*. What followed was more dancing and singing throughout the night. The ritual included a mock battle, pipe smoking, speeches, and a marriage.

The Apaches set up a new tipi and ensconced Romero in it with a virgin maiden. As any normal man would do, when his ego had been so inflated, Romero deflowered the woman. Afterwards, the Apaches daubed his chest and face with her blood. They tied a white feather in his curly black hair, a feather he later always wore attached to his hat.

The problem was...he swaggered. The little head was still doing the thinking for the big head. If he had not swaggered so much, his antics on the plains might have be retold around campfires for awhile and forgotten. But word of his unsanctioned marriage reached the office of the zealous *Custos* Posada nearly before Romero had returned to Santa Fe. Perhaps it was the word of *El Carpentiero*, who was offended by Romero's gloating.

Posada accused him of participating in a heathen marriage, which Romero denied. He did admit trading a knife for sex but, he claimed, no marriage had ever taken place.

The Inquisition found Romero guilty and sentenced him to service in a slave galley in the Philippines. He pleaded for mercy and, perhaps in a moment of compassion, the inquisitors commuted the harsh sentence to banishment from New Mexico.

End of story. Right? Lesson learned? Not for Romero, who still hadn't begun using his big head.

Six years later, under the name of Diego Pérez de Salazar, he married a *mestiza* in Guanajuato, Mexico. The problem was, he had a legal wife in New Mexico. Before he could recite a *"Hail Mary!"* he was convicted of polygamy by the Inquisition in Mexico City and confined to its *cárceles secretas,* or secret prison.

His punishment included being marked with an insignia of a bigamist and crowned with a conical hat. With a noose around his neck and carrying a wax candle, he was paraded through the streets behind a crier. His penance included 200 lashes while he walked and a sentence of six years' labor on a galley slave.

While waiting to ship out enslaved on his first galley, Diego Romero died in jail in Veracruz on October 23, 1678.

One is led to wonder whether he ever figured out how to reverse the process so his big head could do his thinking.

Doña Teresa — Crypto-Jew or Victim?
Spanish Inquisition tries the Governor's wife

In the Spanish Colony of Nuevo México in 1663, Doña Teresa de Aguilera y Roche, wife of Governor Bernardo López de Mendizábal, was accused by the Spanish Inquisition of being a Crypto-Jew. She and her husband, who also had been accused, were arrested, shackled, and hauled to Mexico City for trial.

In 1492, the year Columbus sailed the "ocean blue," the Spanish Inquisition had been in force for 14 years. King Ferdinand and Queen Isabella issued a decree that same year, ordering all Jews and Muslims in Spain to convert or leave. The intent of the decree was to eliminate Crypto-Jews, who practiced their faith in secret, from *conversos* — converts who practiced Christianity and, more specifically, Catholicism. Of approximately 80,000 Jews and 200,000 *conversos* in Spain, about 40,000 chose to emigrate. Some arrived in northern New Mexico, whose remoteness and distance from both Mexico City and Spain offered respite from the long arm of the Inquisition.

Historian Thomas Madden has written, "The Inquisition was not born out of a desire to crush diversity and oppress people. It was an attempt to stop unjust executions. Yes, you read that correctly. Heresy was a crime against the state." However, the practice of the Inquisition was quite different. Envious people, with their own agendas, often falsely accused others, who died at the hands of the executioner, or worse — if acquitted — lost all their possessions.

The question here is whether Doña Teresa was a Crypto-Jew or a victim of colonial politics.

Ever since Don Juan de Oñate led a group north from Mexico City to establish a colony, the governor and military clashed with the Franciscan friars. The governor paid the king of Spain for the right to serve as head of the colony. He then had to find a way to recoup his investment and also make enough profit to live in leisure the rest of his life. Since the Spanish had found no gold, as they had in Mexico and Peru, New Mexican governors used the military to compel the indigenous people to work on their behalf, virtually enslaving them. Governors mostly were cruel and ruthless in their endeavor.

Priests, meanwhile, struggled to curtail the greed and oppression of the governor, while they also sought to convert people of Christianity. However, to do this, they required a church — not just a small chapel but an edifice reminiscent of the churches they knew in Spain. They also required a *convento,* or residence, in which to live, servants, farmers, herdsmen, attendants at Mass, and financial contributions for their maintenance. Their abuse of the indigenous people was no less offensive than that of the governor.

When Doña Teresa arrived in Santa Fe, local people took note. She came from a world and social class quite different from anyone most Santa Feans would have encountered. She had been born in Tuscany to an Irish mother and Spanish father. She was well educated, read books, and spoke several languages — something most women in Santa Fe could not claim. Her behavior planted seeds of discord that festered into envy and hatred.

When Governor López de Mendizábal, issued an order prohibiting the Franciscan priests from forcing the local people to work if they were not paid a salary and recognized their right to practice their ceremonial dances and religion, he ran afoul of ecclesiastical officials. That may have been all that was needed to incite the malicious envy of clergy, citizens, and servants at the Palace of the Governors and get his wife and him arrested. They were jailed at the nearby Santa Domingo Pueblo and then transported separately the 1600-mile length of *El Camino Real de Tierra Adentro* (the Royal Road of the Interior) to Mexico City.

Doña Teresa was accused by household staff of being cruel, uncharitable, and harsh. Swept up with others for secretly practicing Jewish rituals, she had 41 counts brought against her.

Her accusers claimed she locked herself in her chambers on Friday evenings, ostensibly for privacy, while she bathed, washed her hair, cut her nails, and changed her linen. She didn't wash any other day, so obviously she was preparing for the Hebrew Sabbath the next day. That was proof she was *judaizanta,* a Jew.

She kept foreign and unintelligible books and papers in locked drawers in her quarters, although none of the maids and servants in the Palace of the Governors could have read them if they could have had access to them. In any event, they thought, she could have read books written in Spanish. This, and the fact she laughed while reading these books, showed them to be heretical. Therefore, she must be a Jew.

She and the governor drank chocolate on Good Friday in 1661, and she ate toast from a special loaf, as if the bread was part of a Jewish ritual. They were also accused failing to abstain from eating on holy days as proof of their heresy.

The list goes on and on. There were charges for failing to observe the usual religious practices, such as invoking the Virgin Mary for intercession, devotion to any saint, chastising servants for carrying rosaries, and failure to inspire the fear of God in the household staff. There were charges of gossiping and speaking ill of priests, of practicing witchcraft, and of acts suppressed with malice that could only have come from observing forbidden Judaic ceremonies.

She was even accused of hurling insults at friars when en route to Mexico City, although her fury stemmed from seeing her husband's prison cart as they wound they way along El Camino Real. This accusation was proof, at least to the prosecutor, of her spiritual imperfection and failure to see she would not have been arrested unless the Tribunal of the Holy Office of the Inquisition believed she had committee sins.

In prison in Mexico City, Doña Teresa was billed for the thread and fabric she requested, for the chocolate she took for relaxation, for housekeeping, laundry, and even coal. She also asked for paper and pen and wrote a defense against each of the 41 charges.

For two years, she fought against her accusers; for two years, she lived in the prison and shuttled between her cell and the courtroom. She was assigned an attorney, Don Jose de Cabrera, but, when she learned he had represented plaintiffs against her husband, she replaced him with Don Alonzo de Alayes Pinelo.

Her written defense was highly literate, bringing to bear logic, memory, belief, and passion to expose the corruption in the colony and insight into the motivation of her detractors. She wrote, if witnesses falsely testified against her husband and her, it was from a conspiracy between Don Diego de Peñalosa, the governor who replaced López de Mendizábal, and the friars, who were driven by their lust for power and greed.

She refuted each of the charges of heresy brought against her. Among her arguments was one about washing her hair. She said there was no significance in washing her hair on Friday or any particular day. It took two days for her to complete her coiffure, she said, claiming she suffered from pain in her arms. And, of course, she wanted to look her best on Sunday when she attended Mass.

After two years of legal battling, Doña Teresa's case was finally suspended without either conviction or acquittal in 1664. Her husband, age 43, did not fare as well. He had died in his dank prison cell.

Bernardo Gruber—*El Alémán*
How the *Jornada del Muerto* got its name

During Christmas 1668, Bernardo Gruber, a German peddler plying his trade from Mexico City to Santa Fe, was at the Quarai pueblo, a few miles north of today's Mountainair. Quarai is one of three pueblos, along with Ábo and Gran Quivira, which make up the Salinas Pueblo Missions National Monument. The Franciscans in the 1600s built mission churches at these three pueblos, among others, but Quarai was where the Holy Office of the Inquisition was based. It was not a good place to do what Gruber did.

Gruber, called *El Alémán* (the German) by his friends, had celebrated the *posadas* during the fiesta, following the last journey of the Holy Family in search of an inn, the way nearly all Europeans in the Southwest did. He got drunk. Then everyone attended Christmas Eve Mass, fulfilling the church's requirement for one of its holy days.

Sitting in the choir loft with his friend Juan Sarrano, the inebriated Gruber whispered secretively to choir members. If they ate the slips of paper he had, they would be free from harm, whether caused by knife or shot, for 24 hours. The slips had collections of letters written on them, like X ABNA X AKNA X. Gruber may not have understood the idea behind these typical "magic squares" of German folk magic.

Apparently the Inquisition tribunal didn't understand them either, but that was no reason not to charge him with witchcraft. The charge was substantiated when Juan Nieto ate one of the papers, was pricked first with an awl, then a knife, and yet remained uninjured. Despite the apparent validity of the magic, Nieto recanted the witchcraft and turned Gruber in.

Fray Juan de Paz, agent and *custos* of the Inquisition, arrested and imprisoned Gruber. According to the Franciscan rules, the *custos* had to find the correct number of witnesses, as dictated by church law, to convict the German. That proved difficult. No one liked the Inquisition nor trusted Fray Paz. In fact, most lived in fear of the ecclesiastical tribunal and its use of torture to extract confessions.

Gruber remained imprisoned for 27 months. By then, he had had enough.

During his incarceration, he was served by Atanasio, an Apache youth, who brought his meals. Gruber worked a deal with the boy — help him escape and he would take Atanasio with him so he could return to his people. He broke the window in his cell by pushing out the heavy wooden bars. With the aid of Atanasio, they escaped and fled at night with five horses and one gun. Skirting the Oscura Mountains to the east, they headed south on *El Camino Real de Tierra Adentro* (the Royal Road of the Interior Land) traversing the waterless desert we call the *Jornada del Muerto*. It wasn't named that the night Gruber wandered into it.

When the Spanish learned he had escaped, they pursued him, intent on recapturing or killing him.

After a harrowing ride into the desolate desert track, the two men found themselves parched and exhausted. At a place called *Las Peñuelas*, Gruber sent Atanasio ahead to find water. There were only seeps in the hills, and what water the springs provided didn't flow very far. It you wanted water, you had to look for it.

When Atanasio returned, *El Alémin* and one horse were gone. The Apache servant tried to find Gruber, but he was unsuccessful. One may presume, the boy believed Gruber had continued on without him. Atanasio surrendered to the friars at *Senecú*, a pueblo near today's Socorro. The Spanish searched in vain, never finding Gruber. He had made his getaway. Or had he?

Later in the summer of 1670, travelers making their way toward Socorro came upon the skeleton of a horse tethered to a lonely tree. Nearby they found some clothing and hank of hair. Farther on they found a skull and bones that had been gnawed by animals. Fray Paz assumed these were the remains of Gruber and closed the case. God, it seemed, had seen fit to punish *El Alémin* for his sacrilege.

In Mexico City, convinced of his death, the Inquisitors auctioned Gruber's wares and ordered Mass be said for the repose of his soul. The bones, having been gathered in the desert and shipped south, were buried in the church cemetery.

One has to ask, did Gruber's Apache companion murder him for the horses and the arquebus he had stolen during his escape? If so, why would he have left one horse behind? Just as puzzling is the question of why Atanasio would have surrendered to the Spanish who'd been seeking him, unless of course he had first disposed of the booty?

El Alémán was not the first to die in the Jornada nor would he be the last. But it was his death apparently that gave this stretch of El Camino Real its gruesome name. How many people died along the Jornada del Muerto is unknown, although the number of deaths can be measured in dozens, if not hundreds.

John Kissell in his book, *Kiva, Cross & Crown*, ends his telling of the tale this way: "Although the life of this luckless German wanderer has long been forgotten, his death gave name to, or at least reinforced the name, of the Jornada del Muerto, the Dead Man's Route."

If you go in search of El Alémán, that point of interest along El Camino Real, you'll leave Interstate 25 at Upham and venture north on a county highway. Eventually the railroad tracks run east from the hills of Radium Springs and soon parallel the road. A former railroad dispatcher had posted on the Internet there was a sign saying Alémán at mile marker 1056. You can keep track of those from your car, and soon you'll come to one with 1056 on it. You won't find an Alémán sign nor the short siding the dispatcher had referenced. Apparently the railroad has been rebuilt since he posted his information.

Instead you'll found Spaceport America, located in what is now known as Alémán arroyo. El Camino Real runs north and south about halfway between the Spaceport's gate and the county road connecting Upham to Engle.

As you walk the land where Gruber may have died, you may think he'd probably be happy to know the newest adventurers, and maybe peddlers, will be embarking on journeys into the unknown just as he did from the point where his life ended. Hopefully, they will have a more successful venture.

The Two Narbonas
Protecting the Diné homeland

The Chuska Mountains lay across New Mexico and Arizona between Farmington and Gallup. For centuries, an east-west canyon eroded through layers of sandstone, just north of today's Window Rock, served as the only pass through the mountains.

The Diné, whom we call Navajo, referred to the pass as *Beesh Lichii'ii Bigiizh* or Copper. They used it when they left their homes in Canyon de Chelly to raid Spanish settlements along the Rio Grandé. The Spanish, and later Mexicans, used the pass to attack the Diné in their canyon stronghold.

This is the story of two men—both named Narbona, although not related to each other—and how the pass came to be named after one of them.

The Diné were nomadic hunter-gatherers, who migrated into the Four Corners region around 1400 CE. They were cousins to Athabaskan people we call Eskimos. As they settled into their Southwestern homes, they acquired weaving, farming, and other cultural aspects from nearby Pueblo people.

They traded when times were good and raided when they were not. Their warlike nature helped define the northern limit of Spanish expansion, following Coronado, Oñate, and others.

In 1804, the Diné raided the Spanish outpost at Cebolletta, north of Laguna Pueblo in the shadow of Mount Taylor. The Diné called the mountain *tsoodził* or turquoise. It was one of their four sacred mountains lost to the Spanish, along with grazing land they'd wanted to retrieve.

In retaliation for their raid, Lieutenant Colonel Antonio Narbona—the first of our two men so named—led a contingent of Spanish soldiers in 1805 through the pass and into Canyon de Chelly. There his soldiers killed 115 Navajo and captured 33 women and children, whom they sold into slavery.

It was a time of fragile peace, often shattered. Thirty years later, after Mexican independence, raids and counter raids continued. In February 1835, Blas de Hinojos, *Camadante General de Nuevo México*, led nearly 1,000 Mexican troops west from Santa Fe on a slaving expedition. It was the largest armed expedition Spain or Mexico had ever sent against the Navajo Nation.

He planned to use the 8,000-foot-high canyon to access Canyon de Chelly. However, before Hinojos reached his objective, Diné scouts spotted the dust cloud of the Mexicans crossing the Chaco Wash. Their polished buttons reflected sunlight like mirrors, costing them their advantage of surprise.

Chief Narbona — the second of this name — led 250 warriors into the pass and hid them high in the rocky defile. They waited until the Mexicans entered the canyon which was so steep and narrow they had to lead their horses on foot. When the owl-hoot signal was given, the Diné rained arrows and shoved boulders down on the unprotected troops. Those with rifles fired on them. They killed the Mexicans, like — as Narbona said — cutting a long tree trunk into kindling.

A few years later, after the U.S. had wrested control of territory from Mexico, Colonel John Washington led a force into Navajo country. The United States was bent on achieving the peace that had eluded the Spanish and Mexicans. They met with Diné envoys who agreed to discuss a settlement. Led by Narbona and José Largo, another chief, the Diné brought sheep and horses as gifts.

During the peace talks, the Americans accused one of the Diné of stealing a horse. Angry at the charge, the Diné prepared to leave. Then, one of Washington's troops fired on them, killing six, including the 82-year-old Narbona, whose ill-health had made it a struggle for him to attend the conference. Another of the soldiers scalped the chief, claiming his long, white hair as a trophy.

What followed was nearly constant warfare until General James Carlton's mission to remove the Diné from their traditional homeland and march them nearly 400-miles in winter to Bosque Redondo. This disastrous episode ended in 1868, when the treaty was signed by General William T. Sherman, Diné Chief Barboncito, and 28 other Diné headmen, including Narbona Segundo, presumably a descendant of the old chief.

The treaty put an end to hostilities between the Diné and the Americans, who turned their attention to subduing the Apache and other tribes.

The Americans named the pass after John Washington, and it remained that way for decades. The Diné never forgot about the murder of their chief, but in time—after several generations—they forgot after whom the pass was named.

In 1990, students of the Navajo Community College in Shiprock learned the Washington for whom the pass had been named wasn't George, our first President, but John, the colonel who had caused the trouble leading to The Long Walk. They became indignant about having an important location in the Navajo Nation named after an enemy and began a campaign to change it.

On December 10, 1992, the United States Board on Geographic Names voted unanimously in favor of changing the name Washington Pass to Narbona Pass. It was perhaps the first time in their history the Diné defied their culture and broke with tradition of never repeating the name of the deceased, insisting the canyon be named after the long-dead, but esteemed chief.

Bernardo Abeyta—Founder of Chimayó
Chapel of the "Holy Dirt"

For the deeply religious, El Santuario de Chimayó is a sacred destination. For others, the journey is a trip back in time. It is also the story of Bernardo Abeyta.

Chimayó is about ten miles east of Española, north of Santa Fe, in the shadow of the Sangre de Cristo mountains.

The village predates the sanctuary by nearly two centuries, but it is the sanctuary which draws people to this day.

The story of Chimayó begins shortly after the Pueblo Revolt of the 1680s. Spanish settlers began farming the fertile Chimayó Valley. While some tilled the land, others of these hard working, independent people were engaged in weaving and stock raising. Most hoped to earn the noble title of *hidalgo* along with the land they worked. Frequently, they were granted land and farming implements to create what remained a life of hardship on the frontier.

By the 1740s, the village was prosperous enough to gain the attention of marauding Indians and Spanish outlaws. Security was so critical, the villagers built a plaza fortified by constructing adobe buildings side-by-side. The Plaza of San Buenaventura, as it was called, had but two entrances and also a defensive watch tower, or *torreon*. The lifeblood of the village, its *acequia madre* (or mother ditch), ran through the plaza, now called *Plaza del Cerro*. With water, food, and thick walls, the people of Chimayó could avoid the worse scourges of their time.

And so life went on for some 70 years.

Around 1810, as the traditional story goes, Don Bernardo Abeyta, a member in of the *Hermandad de Nuestro Padre Jesús el Nazareno* (Penitentes), was performing the customary penances on Good Friday when he saw an unusual light around the hills of El Potrero. He sought out the light and found it was coming from the ground. Upon digging in the earth, he uncovered a crucifix, which he named the miraculous crucifix of Our Lord of Esquipulas.

The crucifix was removed to Santa Cruz, the nearest church but was missing the next day. It was later found in its original location. This strange phenomenon occurred three times, convincing villagers the cross was meant to remain in Chimayó. So, Don Abeyta and the villagers built a small chapel, which they named Christ of Esquipulas. Then, as the story continues, the miraculous healing began. So many claimed to be healed, Abeyta petitioned Fr. Sebastián Álvarez, the parish priest of the church in Santa Cruz, to build a bigger church next to the chapel so the villagers could hear Mass.

It took six years, but eventually Francisco Fernández Valetín, vicar general of the Diocese of Durango, granted permission, and the present church was built alongside the small chapel. The people named their new church *El Santuario de Nuestra Señor de Esquipulas*.

This building has remained in use for more than 100 years. The sanctuary was a privately owned chapel until the year 1929. Carmen Abeyta de Chaves, Abeyta's daughter, inherited the property when her father died. Despite attempts to force her to give it to the church, she kept it. Donations from pilgrims were a major source of income for her. Maria de los Angeles Chaves, Carmen's daughter, inherited it next and was owner until 1915.

In 1929, when the family was in financial trouble, members of the Spanish Colonial Arts Society purchased the sanctuary and donated it to the Archdiocese of Santa Fe.

Believed to be built on sacred earth with miraculous healing powers, the Santuario de Chimayó is probably the most visited church in New Mexico. The crucifix still resides on the chapel alter, but it is the curative powers of *El Posito*, the sacred sand pit, that people now seek. Each year during Holy Week, thousands of people make a pilgrimage to Chimayó to visit the sanctuary and take away a bit of sand from the pit. Pilgrims walk a few yards or a hundred miles, often completing the last stretch of the journey on their knees, and many have claimed to be cured of diseases and infirmities. The walls of the chapel are hung with discarded crutches and before-and-after photos as testaments to the healing.

Beyond the religious significance of the chapel, the sanctuary is a repository of some of the most remarkable *Reredos*, or sacred paintings, and *Butlos*, or sacred carvings, in New Mexico. The Reredos were painted in the early 1800s by Molleno, also known as The Chili Painter, by José Aragon of nearby Cordova, and by Miguel Aragon. Each is resplendent in figures and symbols that teach as well as compel reverence.

Known as the "Lourdes of America," El Santuario, with its ancient adobe walls and bell towers, has the appearance of a quaint, humble mission chapel, but one that draws nearly 30,000 visitors a year. They come to worship, to ask for peace in the world and in their hearts, to fulfill a promise, and to feel the healing touch of God.

Chimayó's El Santuario was registered as a national historic landmark in 1970.

Mexican Period
1821-1846

Maria Gertrudis Barceló—*La Tules*
What price respect?

General Stephen Watts Kearney paced the length of the small, musty reception room in the 250-year-old Governor's Palace in Santa Fe. He had marched his Army of the West into the New Mexican provincial capital a week before. His conquest came without having fired a shot, which he'd considered a formidable achievement, especially since his 1,700-man army had completed its 750-mile journey from Fort Leavenworth, leaving it weary and unprepared to encounter the expected Mexican militia of 2,000. Instead of the confrontation, he was met by Governor Manuel Armijo, who surrendered and then climbed into his carriage, making a hasty retreat toward Mexico City.

Now the general needed financing to continue carrying the battle to the Mexicans, supporting General John Fremont in California. He needed food, ammunition, and uniforms. Colonel Alexander Dohiphan was Kearney's second in command and would assume the governorship after Kearney marched west. When Kearney asked his colleague if he had seen the condition of his men's boots, Doniphan inquired whether he'd heard from Fort Leavenworth. Had Congress approved any finances? The answer, of course, was no.

Kearney considered his predicament. The church offered no funds. It was opposed to Armijo's leaving, priests having had it too good for too long. Business leaders and ranchers were only too happy to see the former governor depart. They had much more positive prospects for more trade and even more wealth, but they were a tight-fisted bunch who hadn't made their fortunes outfitting armies.

Not liking to go hat-in-hand, Doniphan nevertheless made the rounds—again—to the business leaders: the mercantile owners, freighters, financiers, anyone who had two coins to rub together. He couldn't understand their reticence. New Mexico was now a territory of the United States. These men were freed from the tyrannical, burdensome rule of Mexico City. Their avenues of commerce were broader. Straighter. Open to trade from the east—unrestricted trade promising more merchandise, more rapidly, with higher margins and greater profit. He wondered where their loyalty lay.

That night, frustrated and disheartened, Doniphan dined at La Fonda Hotel with some junior officers. As the men talked, he watched the maitre d'hotel seat Samuel and Susan Magoffin. They had ridden into Santa Fe the day after Samuel's brother James, who had arrived earlier, had negotiated Armijo's surrender. Seeing the freighter and his young bride gave the colonel an idea.

Doniphan didn't particularly want to ask Magoffin to underwrite the army, although if the freighter had chosen to do that, he was fairly certain they'd later be able to get the Secretary of War to reimburse him. He was looking for an introduction to any Santa Fean who would be inclined to render assistance.

Much to everyone's surprise, Susan Magoffin, who considered herself the first white woman ever to trek the Santa Fe Trail and *El Camino Real de Tierra Adentro* (the Royal Road of the Interior Land), recommended Maria Gertrudis Barceló. A cunning businesswoman, Barceló ran the most successful tavern and hostelry in Santa Fe. She was a gambler whose five-card monte game was popular but suspect—and worse she was reputed to operate a bordello on her property. But she was known to have a hoard of cash, which she frequently loaned to soldiers at usurious rates.

Everyone, including the officers of the newly arrived army, knew Doña Barceló preferred to be called *La Tules*, after the slender, flowering reeds found along streams. Those less kind called her that because of the sensuous way she swayed her hips as she walked.

The next day, Doniphan called on Maria Barceló. Before their meeting, he had inquired about the Santa Fean many considered notorious. She had been born in the tiny village of Tomé, 30 miles south of Albuquerque. She was married and had had two sons, both of whom died in infancy. The loss of her children changed her. She abandoned her roll as mother and assumed that of a businesswoman. Since Doniphan could learn nothing of her husband, he presumed she had also abandoned her roll as wife, although she remained married. Her husband just did not figure into her plans. She was literate. She was shrewd. And she was successful, amassing wealth and power. Still, people whispered behind her back, saying her hotel and tavern were a front for her brothel. Her gambling was crooked. She was even accused of fleecing men in her establishment who had drunk themselves into a stupor.

Maria Gertrudis Barceló claimed the title doña. Her family background sustained the honorific. The people of Santa Fe snickered at her use of it. When Doniphan arrived, she knew exactly why he was there, although she made him explain General Kearney's plight and make his request.

She led him into the courtyard of her home, yet remained silent as they walked through the gardens. Doniphan was patient. He knew he had asked a lot of this woman. He knew she now pondered her answer. The tinkling of water cascading in the fountain and the chirping of birds were the only sounds disturbing their walk.

Doña Barceló stopped and faced the colonel. She knew a good thing when she saw it. For too long, rumors about her whispered around Santa Fe like breezes ruffling leaves in cottonwoods around the plaza. The army was her opportunity to gain what she most desired — an end to the gossip muttered behind lace fans. If it aided the army's war effort, so much the better. American or Mexican made no difference to her. Both had money to spend and did so to her profit.

Finally, she agreed, and a deal was struck. She would outfit the general's army, and Doniphan would help *La Tules* gain her objective.

When Doniphan reported to Kearney, the general was puzzled over a singular condition. Why, he asked, did this woman want him to throw a ball? As it was explained to him, Doniphan now enlightened the general.

Santa Feans loved fandangos. Ladies dressed in silk and satin gowns that left their arms and necks bare and their bosoms exposed. They walked boldly, swishing their ruffled skirts with graceful oscillation. They did not seem to know what modesty was. But they loved to dance. So, Kearney had to throw a ball for Doña Barceló.

Although Kearney was incredulous, if this astute woman wanted him to dance for his money, he would bury his pride and do it. Invitations to what the general was calling his Victory Ball were sent to every prominent family in Santa Fe. It did not matter if the date conflicted with anyone's plans. No one in Santa Fe would miss this night.

The ballroom at La Fonda Hotel was lavishly appointed. Candles in wall sconces and chandeliers reflected in strategically placed mirrors, designed especially to cast soft, golden light throughout the room. At one end of the ballroom, tables held the delicacies of New Mexico and a sommelier poured fragrant wines and champagne. At the other end, the army band played and, despite their limited array of instruments, managed a cheerful sound.

Everyone who was anyone in Santa Fe arrived. They came in twos, in small groups, even officers who had no escorts but wanted to enjoy the festivity. They all waited for the general, who soon made his entrance with the Magoffins.

Kearney was dressed in his Class A uniform with its custom-tailored blouse and gold-braid epaulets. His boots gleamed from the high polish his valet had applied. He wore his ceremonial sword with its ornate, silver guard rather than the steel weapon he carried into battle. Magoffin, as usual, was dressed in black broadcloth. It was his custom, but this night he chose his suit so as not to detract from his wife.

The mistress of the Magoffin home entered the ballroom wearing a blue, floor-length silk gown with a fashionable bustle and a modest train. The dress had long sleeves and a high, lace collar. Susan Magoffin was just too proper a woman to expose her arms and shoulders as the Mexican women did. While her gown was nearly as dark as her husband's suit, she had draped a red, crepe Chinese shawl around her shoulder. One always wanted a bit of color. She scanned the room, noting most of the women's gowns exposed bosoms and so much cleavage Susan covered her face with her shaw to hide her blush.

Doniphan, a big-boned, lumbering man, bowed to Susan and ask her to dance. *La Tules* had not yet arrived, awaiting the pregnant moment when every eye would be upon her. Susan replied by placing her hand in his and allowed him to lead her to the dance floor. They made quite a couple—he being a couple inches above six feet, while she barely exceeded five feet.

The band played a *cuna*, or cradle, a strange kind of frontier waltz. Doniphan and Magoffin wrapped their arms around each other's waists and leaned back. In time to the music, they rocked back and forth in a swinging embrace, mimicking a cradle. Samuel Magoffin and Kearney watched as Doniphan whirled Susan around the dance floor and return her to her husband when the music ended.

Then, at the colonel's signal, the band struck up a processional march, while Stephen Watts Kearney, general of the United States Army of the West, escorted Doña Maria Gertrudis Barceló into the ballroom. She wore a crimson taffeta gown that exposed her bosom and short, puffed sleeves set off her shoulders. The gown's skirt fell straight to the floor and had a ruffled hem that gave it the appearance of a bell. The taffeta rustled as she walked. Doña Maria adorned herself with three chains of heavy gold, the longest of which ended in a crucifix inlaid with precious stones, perhaps an heirloom dating to Spanish mission times, although not an heirloom of Barceló's family.

There was an audible gasp when Doña Barceló entered. The center of attention on the arm of undoubtedly the most powerful man in the West, she carried herself erect, swaying coquettishly, with a devilish twinkle in her eye. The silence that followed could be found only in a mausoleum on a moonless night. Even the band faltered, garnering a stern look from Doniphan. Silently reprimanded, the band leader refocused his players and kept the processional bright and cheerful. Doña Maria beamed and nodded to anyone who caught her attention.

When the general and lady in red reached the center of the room, the band began playing a formal waltz. They began to dance. Encouraged by Doniphan, who led off, the officers applauded and so drew everyone else in the room into the ovation.

Kearney held himself erect and formally led his partner around the floor. Enjoying herself beyond anything she could have imagined — and she could imagine a great deal — Doña Maria laughed and twirled on the general's arm as if she were quicksilver he somehow had to contain. The notorious tavern keeper, gambler, and madam of Santa Fe — a politically astute woman, who had frequently influenced deals, although in anonymity — was now the center of Santa Fe's society. It was the moment she had craved. This night. This moment. Now, at least momentarily, she had the attention, if not the respect, of every woman who previously had snickered behind her back. She knew she'd be the talk of the town for weeks to come, talk that would follow a different tack than earlier.

Two weeks following the ball, later than he had wanted, General Kearney led his troops west from Santa Fe, toward Fremont and the Californians engaging the Mexican army at Los Angeles. The army's wagons were loaded with food and other necessary supplies, enough to carry them across the width of the New Mexican territory and Mojave Desert. The troops even had new boots.

Only Doña Maria Gertrudis Barceló knew the price the U.S. government had paid.

New Mexico Territorial Period

1847-1912

Edward Beale — Camel Driver
Will that be one hump or two?

Visit El Moro National Monument near Grants and you'll find the name P. Gilmer Breckinridge carved in Inscription Rock. Except for its remarkable typography, there's nothing unusual about the inscription; the soft, sandstone cliff has hundreds of petroglyphs and names carved in it, including Juan de Oñate, the Spanish colonist who founded a New Mexico colony in 1598.

Breckenridge traveled with Lieutenant Edward Fitzgerald Beale, in charge of 25 camels accompanying the Beale party that was upgrading a wagon road from Santa Fe to California.

You'll also find Beale's name carved in the cliff face. This is his story.

From 1846 to 1848, the Mexican-American War was fought to determine who controlled the Southwest. Beale was with General Stephen Kearny battling *Californio* lancers. American Dragoons had engaged the *Californios* in the Battle of San Pasqual and had been soundly beaten. Now, encamped atop Mule Hill with his wounded and exhausted troops, Kearny realized they would be decimated if they were attacked again. His only recourse was to send men on foot through the ranks of the enemy to San Diego, where Commodore Robert Stockton had reinforcements.

Beale, along with Kit Carson and a Dieguerno Indian, volunteered to attempt the 15-mile journey. Hampton Sides tells the story in his book, *Blood and Thunder.* The three men slid down the scree of Mule Hill. Because their boots made so much noise, they took them off and hooked them under their belts. They left their clanking canteens behind, too.

At one point, they came upon a *Californio* lancer on guard, who took his time to smoke a cigaret before turning his horse and riding away from men hiding nearby.

Beale and Carson had lost their boots in the dark. Now their feet were lacerated by rocks and punctured by cactus spines. The Indian's moccasins had faired only little better. Still they pushed on, for three days, taking separate routes to ensure one of them would get through.

When Beale reached Stockton, he was dehydrated and so exhausted he was delirious, but he reported Kearny's dilemma. It would take him a month in the infirmary aboard the USS Congress to recover.

We all know the outcome of the war and subsequent Gadsden Purchase. The United States pushed its southern border from near Colorado to its present location, acquiring 900,000 square miles of territory, an addition about the size of Europe.

A decade after the American victory, Edward Beale — having resigned his Naval commission — was contracted by John B. Floyd, Secretary of War for President Buchanan, to improve the 35th Parallel wagon road. During the war, the road originally had been blazed by the Mormon Battalion, organized by Lieutenant Colonel Philip St. George Cooke (for whom the mountains north of Deming are named). Beale was assigned the task of building a road across New Mexico to California. Another group of surveyors and contractors would later build a stretch from Fort Smith, Arkansas, to Santa Fe, completing the 1200-mile-long federal highway. Unbeknownst to Beale, the contract required him to take part of the camel herd with him.

Camels in the American Southwest seemed like a good idea. The region's punishing climate and terrain took a terrible toll on horses and mules upon which the army had always depended. Proponents of camels said they were stronger, patient in loading and unloading, and tolerant of little food, water, or rest. Their feet were well suited for grassy or sandy plains, as well as rough, rocky and hilly paths, and they required no shoeing.

The argument convinced the U.S. Congress to appropriate $30,000 [more than $800,000 in today's currency] to obtain Egyptian and Tunisian camels for an experiment to learn how they fared as pack animals. That was in 1855 and, within a year, Major Henry Wayne had arrived at Camp Verde outside San Antonio, Texas, with 32 dromedary and two Bactrian camels. A second herd brought the number of animals to 70.

Although he was not in favor of the idea of herding camels, Beale accepted responsibility for 25 of them. His road-building expedition left San Antonio on June 25, 1857, heading west through Fort Davis and El Paso, Texas, and then from Albuquerque to Fort Defiance in New Mexico Territory.

If you're checking facts, you might say, "Ah, ha. Fort Defiance was in Arizona." Don't forget, following the Mexican-American War, New Mexico Territory included both what is now Arizona and New Mexico. In actuality, Fort Defiance was on the homeland of the Diné.

Imagine the reaction of Indians to their first sighting of a camel. Many had found the white man an interloper in their homelands. Beale had dispatched a patrol to find water, and it had not returned when expected. Camel drivel Hadji Ali on his camel went in search of them and found the five troopers under attack. With no time to go for help, Ali drew his scimitar and charged, screaming, "*Allahu akbar.*" Facing an olive-brown, turbaned Arab in traditional clothing, shouting in a language none could understand, the Indians fled in terror from the "desert devil." We can only wonder what stories they told in their lodges afterwards.

Along his journey, Beale had a change of opinion about the camels. He found them superior to mules in the desert country. They could go a week without water and foraged on prickly pear and other desert plants along the way, browse a mule wouldn't touch. Each camel could carry a load of up to a thousand pounds, hundreds more than a mule, and, because they remained quietly on their knees, were infinitely easier to pack. Mules didn't like the camels and, therefore, the muleskinners didn't like them either, saying they were foul-smelling, ugly, and evil tempered. In some accounts, you might think the muleskinners were referring to the camel drivers and not their charges.

In his journal, Beale wrote, "They pack water for others for days under a hot sun and never get a drop. They pack heavy burdens of corn and oats for months and never get a grain. They eat worthless shrubs and not only subsist but keep fat. My admiration for the camels increases daily. The harder the test, the more fully they seem to justify all that is said about them."

In his report to the Secretary of War, Beale wrote, "They are the most docile, patient and easily managed creatures in the world, and infinitely more easily worked than mules. From personal observation of the camels, I would rather undertake the management of twenty of them than of five mules. In fact, the camel gives no trouble whatever."

Despite the lack of camaraderie among the animals and their caretakers, Beale's crew of a hundred men surveyed and constructed the ten-foot-wide wagon road. He reached the Colorado River at today's Arizona/California border on October 26, 1857.

Beale wrote of the construction, "It is the shortest route from our western frontier by three hundred miles, being nearly directly west. ... It crosses the great desert, which must be crossed by any road to California, at its narrowest point." It was the most popular road among immigrants in the 1870s and was the foundation for the Santa Fe Railroad and U.S. Route 66. It's still in use today as Interstate 40 running alongside the rails of the Burlington Northern SantaFe Railroad.

So why is there no camel corps in the U.S. Army today?

Although the camel experiment and Beale's use of them proved successful, history eclipsed the results. Four years after he arrived in California, on the opposite side of the continent, secessionists from South Carolina fired on Fort Sumter. America began expending its blood and treasure in a Civil War that dearly tested the will of the people to remain bound as a single nation.

Early in the war, an attempt was made to use the camels to carry mail between Fort Mojave, New Mexico Territory, on the Colorado River and New San Pedro, California, but the attempt was unsuccessful after commanders of both posts objected. They said camels had a nasty personality, bit, spat, and made lots of noise when they walked. These were not the types of things the military could tolerate, especially since the U.S. Army was a horse and mule outfit, whose soldiers did not have the skills to control camels.

Some proponents of the experiment said it failed because it was supported by Jefferson Davis, a Senator from Mississippi and former Secretary of War who left the United States to become President of the Confederate States of America.

In 1864, the army, which had no further interest in the animals, sold them at auction to California ranchers, most probably as a novelty. Beale bought some himself for his Tajon Ranch near Bakersfield.

Though some escaped into the wild, the camels were simply forgotten. The last of the animals was reportedly seen in Arizona in 1891. Perhaps. For years afterwards, astonished travelers would spy what appeared to be a wild camel on the horizon.

Ann White — Depending on Kit Carson
Too little, too late

Kit Carson watched the cavalry riding toward his ranch on Rayado Creek, east of Taos. Major William Grier of the First Dragoons led a detachment of some 50 troopers.

Carson put down the harness he was repairing and welcomed the major.

Grier told him Francis Aubrey had brought a wagon train into Fort Union, explaining how one of his wagons had been attacked by Apache.

James White, a trader from Missouri, had left the train about a 150 miles east of Fort Union, he said. He was using mules, not oxen, and wanted to get to Santa Fe faster.

Carson was galled. Francis Xavier Aubrey had far too much experience along the Santa Fe Trail to let a fool idiot with a single wagon attempt the Cimarron Cutoff alone.

Grier explained Aubrey didn't have a choice. White argued he could make it in five or six days. He thought they were well beyond any threat of Indians. White had his wife and infant girl with him, along with a black servant. He added Aubrey also sent three men to protect them, just in case.

Carson shook his head.

Two days ago, Grier continued, a man from Jémez came into Taos to trade. His people used to live at Cicuyé — used to barter with the Jicarilla when they came to the pueblo. He said he had been trading with a band camped on the plains east of the pueblo and saw a white woman and a baby. Grier had been detached to find her and bring her back.

When Carson asked Grier why he'd come to Rayado, the major explained he'd come to recruit the former colonel. Carson argued he'd retired from the army and had a ranch to look after. Grier removed his hat and wiped the sweat band, waiting for Carson to say his say. Then he informed him he wasn't asking. Grier's commanding officer had ordered Carson to join the troop, telling him the army still found him beholden.

At 39, Carson had had enough of adventure and soldiering. All he wanted was to work his ranch and enjoy his wife, Josefa, and their children. Still, he had no choice and left with the Dragoons.

* * *

The Santa Fe Trail was blazed in 1821 by William Becknell who saw profit in trading goods from back east with people in the northern realms of the Province of Nuevo México. It was closer and easier to haul goods from St. Louis than it was from Mexico City, and New Mexicans hungered for what traders brought west.

Three years after cessation of hostilities in the Mexican-American War, when the United States staked claim to the Southwest from Texas to the Pacific, scores of trains each year crossed the plains. They carried goods valued in the millions. Even with its hardship, exposure, and dangers, the wagon road made many a man wealthy.

Despite the fact the road was free to all who ventured upon it, there were people, notably Comanche, Apache, and unsavory groups of highwaymen—*Asalto al coche*, if they were Mexican, as many were—who demanded tolls, part of the train's bounty. Pay the bounty and the wagons could pass. To refuse brought retribution and that usually meant death.

That's what happened to James White, who had driven a few days ahead of Aubrey and the rest of the train. White encountered a band of Jicarilla who demanded gifts. He was an arrogant, stubborn man. How else could a man be described who left the safety of the wagon train? He saw the haggard Apache band as "filthy savages," and refused to pay. Insulted, the Jicarilla left. White must have felt pretty good about the way he put these Apaches in their place.

But they returned in larger numbers—more than a hundred braves. Once more they demanded recompense. Once more White refused. This time threatening the Apache with rifles. The Jicarilla answered the only way they knew. Several braves shot arrows into White from close range. Others killed the men guarding the trader and his family. Ann White and her infant daughter, as well as her servant, were scooped off the wagon and carried away.

That was October. Now it was late November.

* * *

With Carson at his side, Major Grier led his men east along the Cimarron Cutoff of Santa Fe Trail, the route the White family had taken. A few days out, they found the massacre site. The burned wagon was nothing but a pile of charred rubble. Trunks had been smashed open and pillaged, the Jicarilla looking for trophies they could carry back to camp—or perhaps a treasure that would find favor with a wife or win a woman for a man. The mules, of course, were the real treasure, the mark of wealth for those who lived on the plains. They were too valuable to be destroyed and had been claimed as bounty. The Jicarilla would ride them until they were worn out and then eat them. Mule steaks were considered a delicacy. Grier ordered his men to bury the victims.

Carson had seen this too many times. He watched the troopers dig shallow graves in the coarse ground beneath the tough root web of sod.

The troop left fresh graves covered with rocks to keep wolves from finishing off the already partially consumed corpses. They continued east, Carson reading sign for 40 miles. He had an easy, if slow, time of it. There were hoof prints from unshod ponies as well as the stolen mules, whose hooves were shod in iron. There were moccasin tracks, bent grass, overturned rocks. The Jicarilla had made no effort to cover their trail, thinking either they constituted an impregnable force or no one cared enough about White to follow them.

November on the northern *Llano Estacado* is blustery. It often snows, as it did now, obscuring the trail the soldiers had been following. Still, Grier pressed eastward. His men, even in their great coats, were chilled to the bone. Their grumbling harmonized with the unceasing wind.

They came upon a camp abandoned so long ago not even the coals of campfires held any heat. A soldier brought a petticoat to Grier and Carson. It was obviously white woman's clothing, though neither man yet knew what to make of the undergarment lying on the prairie.

The Dragoons rode on. The Jicarilla now knew they were being followed. The band split in two, each going its separate way, a trick frequently used to throw off pursuers or, at least, slow them up. Carson wasn't fooled. He'd seen the trick before. Still, they'd paused to reconnoiter both tracks and decide which to follow.

Grier pondered whether the Apache had gone farther east or maybe turned south. The *Llano*'s no place to be in winter. Maybe they were heading someplace out of the wind and cold. Then an outrider came in with another article of clothing. This time a corded stay.

Carson was certain Ann White was leaving a trail for them to follow—and the direction was east, farther out on the *Llano*. Wind had blown snow off the grasslands in broad patches. Carson found frozen blades of grass bent by a passing foot. He found moccasin tracks, barely visible in the drifting snow. But he found enough sign to lead the troopers to the Jicarilla encampment. They saw the hazy cloud of smoke disbursing in the breeze long before they saw the campfires from which it rose. They'd found the Apache band on the Canadian River near Tucumcari Butte. The Jicarilla didn't know the Dragoons were there...yet.

Carson suggested Grier spread his men out in a wide arc so they could circle around the Apache and surprise them with a trap. Reluctantly, the major concurred, deferring to Carson's much greater experience fighting Indians. With as much stealth as possible, the Dragoons moved out. Soon, they were in position. The Jicarilla had no idea what was about to descend on them, fusillades of rifle fire that would quickly decimate anyone caught in the open. Then a ride through the camp, the calvary swinging the gleaming long blades of their sabers, slicing through muscle and bone until not a single Apache warrior remained.

Carson shouted the order to attack. He charged furiously toward the Apache camp. When he looked over his shoulder, he was astonished. He was alone. Carson pulled up and rode back to Grier, demanding to know why the attack had been called off. Grier had countermanded Carson's order, thinking he'd parlay with the Jicarilla and win Ann White's freedom without bloodshed.

Carson pointed toward the Jicarilla camp and told Grier the Apache would never give up Ann White and her baby without a fight.

The Jicarilla, of course, saw the aborted attack. There would be no surprise, no attempt the drive into camp, creating chaos, and snatching the white woman and her child from the Apache.

Instead, they fanned out, setting a skirmish line to give their women and children a chance to escape the soldiers. While the troopers milled about in confusion, waiting for the major to issue a command, one over-anxious Jicarilla warrior leveled his rifle and fired at Grier. The brave's aim was exceptional, but he was too far away, beyond the killing range of his bullet. The ball lost momentum and power. Another few yards and it would have fallen to earth. Instead, it slammed into Grier's chest, knocking the wind out of him, but it could not even penetrate his wool blouse. All he would show for it was a bruise on his left breast and a band of fleeing Apache.

Carson demanded Grier attack, thinking the major was a much a fool idiot as White had been. The milling horses were reined in and directed toward the camp. The Dragons rode hard, leveling their rifles, firing at any Indian they could see. But they couldn't see many.

The Apache disbursed in every direction, diluting the fire power of the troopers. Like the guerrilla fighters they were, they shot from cover, then ran, creating a delaying action. It had been known for some time, an Apache could lay down next to a clump of grass and be virtually invisible.

It didn't take the women and children long to flee to safety. They scurried behind the slimmest rise of land, lay as still as logs, waiting for the fight to end, for the soldiers to leave. Unlike their other enemies, notably the Comanche, American fighters almost never stopped to loot. They rarely took scalps. They fought furiously, but then the fight went out of them and they left.

Ann White heard the bugler sound charge. She jumped up to see blue-coated soldiers riding toward her. She knew they'd come for her. She screamed and waved, tears streaming down her cheeks. She didn't know if she cried from relief or joy.

The Jicarilla woman guarding her also saw the soldiers. She pushed Ann toward a horse. Ann defied her. The Jicarilla gestured for her to climb on the horse's back. She planned to use it to retain her prisoner and escape the military onslaught.

Ann resisted. When the Apache woman pushed her, she pushed back. They scuffled. The Jicarilla grabbed Ann's hair, trying to drag her to the horse. Ann screamed and fought back, punching the other woman's face. Ann was taller than the Apache. Stronger. Driven by desperate fear.

She broke free of her captor and ran toward the surging Dragoons.

With the short lead Ann got, the Jicarilla woman could easily have caught her, but doing so would have led her away from her mount, toward the charging Dragoons, and certain death. Instead, she grabbed a bow and leveled an arrow at the fleeing woman. She was competent with the weapon; boys had not been the only ones trained to use them. She let the bolt fly as Ann fled. It was an easy shot. The range was short.

The arrow struck Ann in the back, just left of her spine. From 200 yards away, Carson watched. He saw the Apache woman shoot. He saw the white woman lurch as the arrow struck her. He watched her fall face first to earth.

The Jicarilla woman leaped upon her mount and rode hard toward safety, only to be struck in the back by a rifle shot. Her arms flew up above her head, and she toppled backwards off of the horse, landing in the contorted pose of death.

Carson galloped toward Ann, bounding from his horse. But he was too late, if only by moments. Ann White lay dead. The arrow had penetrated her heart. When Carson put his hand on her neck to check her pulse, he found her body still warm.

Kit Carson walked away from the battle. It was over. The Jicarilla that hadn't been killed had fled. He led his horse out onto the grass, away from the troopers. He wanted to be alone. Grier found him there, sitting on the ground, his face covered by his calloused hands.

As Grier approached, Carson looked up. The major was shocked at the expression on Carson's face—an amalgam of anger, dismay, and grief. The dirt on his face was streaked from tears. That surprised Grier even more. The major told him one of his men had found a book in Ann White's hands, hidden beneath her body. He handed the book to him.

Kit Carson looked at the cover, at an image of his alter-ego. It was the dime novel, *Kit Carson: The Prince of the Gold Hunter*, written by Charles Averill. The novelist had emboldened Carson's persona, portraying him as a swashbuckling hero, a man who slaughtered Indians right and left, driving through the storm of battle, to rescue a young girl who'd been kidnapped.

Carson slowly rose to his feet. He turned toward Grier, getting eyeball to eyeball with him, so close the men could feel each other's breath on their faces. Carson told him, if they had attacked when surprise was on their side instead of waiting to parlay, they could have saved Ann.

With that, Carson mounted his horse and rode away, leaving the bewildered major and his Dragoons behind. He rode west toward Rayado Creek. He left the Jicarilla killing field behind him. He left the arrogant major behind him. But he was never able to leave the death of Ann White behind him.

In his final years, living in his Taos' home, Kit Carson worked with a scribbler to write his autobiography. He needed the help, for reading and writing had always been beyond him. The legend of the American West and the writer talked about many of Carson's adventures: his years in the wilderness, his tour of the West during the Mexican-American War, his engagement with the Texas Confederates at Valverde, rounding up Navajo in Canyon de Chelly during The Long Walk.

The writer handed Carson the book, *Kit Carson: The Prince of the Gold Hunter*. He'd pulled it from the shelf where it'd had been ever since Carson returned from the White engagement. He'd kept Ann's copy. It was still smudged and stained from being dragged across New Mexico's northern grasslands.

Carson caressed the book, almost as if it was Ann's hand he held.

"I've often thought," he murmured, "as Miz White read this book, she prayed for my appearance, thinking I'd come and save her."

Carson paused, looking out the window of his adobe, as if he alone saw the woman standing there, her arms outstretched toward him. Awaiting rescue.

"I have much regretted," he sighed, "my failure to save the life of so esteemed a lady."

This story is based on the history written by Hampton Sides, *Blood and Thunder: The Epic Story of Kit Carson and the Conquest of the American West.*

Barboncito — Navajo Chief
Standoff at Tsélaa — Fortress Rock

In 1862, the U.S. government directed General James H. Carlton to round up the Diné, the people we call Navajo, and march them more than 400 miles to Bosque Redondo, in the grasslands of northeast New Mexico. Colonel Kit Carson was assigned the task and, when the Diné resisted leaving their historic — and, to them, sacred — homeland, he enforced a scorched earth policy.

Through the fall of 1863, the Diné watched as their homes were destroyed, their livestock killed, their wells poisoned, and their fields burned. Carson's intended to make it impossible for them to remain in their homeland. He wanted to capture them and march them first to Fort Defiance and from there to Bosque Redondo. But by November only about 200 people had been moved to the reservation.

Part of the core homeland of the Diné is Canyon de Chelly, a canyon cut into the tableland that varies in depth from 600 to 1000 feet. About 12 miles long, it stretches east like a spread-finger hand from Chinle. Two thousand years ago, the canyon was occupied by pueblo people, whose cliff-house ruins dot the walls. The Diné arrived around 1700. It not only sheltered them from harsh weather but also from their enemies. It's the kind of place you wouldn't know is there unless you came upon it suddenly.

In January 1864, Carson dispatched Captain Albert H. Pfeiffer and a hundred troopers to the east end of the canyon, while he and nearly 300 men of the 1st New Mexico Cavalry entered from the west end. Along the way, they destroyed gardens and crops and cut down over 3,000 peach trees that had provided sustenance for the Diné for generations.

The reason Carson was scouring the canyon was because Chief Barboncito, along with Chief Manuelito, had vowed never to surrender to the *bilagaana* or white people. They led nearly 300 of their people into the canyon, and they had prepared well. Women had dried fruit and meat, which the men had cached in the canyon, but they could not avoid the soldiers.

Instead, Barboncito led them to a 700-foot-tall, free-standing butte where the canyon divides into two fingers. The Diné called the rock *Tsélaa*. Today, we call it Fortress Rock.

There are handholds in *Tsélaa* carved by the ancient Puebloans. But imagine scaling a 700-foot cliff face with packs full of food and water, elders in tow, and babies strapped to cradleboards on their mothers' backs. When the cliff became too steep to climb, the Diné propped long ponderosa pine poles against them. They had notched footholds in the logs by which people could climb. Then they pulled the ladders up behind them so their enemies couldn't use them or deny them to the Diné when they wanted to leave.

The army knew they were there. In fact, soldiers fired at the people from the distant edge of the canyon, but it was too far for bullets to carry, and they fell harmlessly into the depths.

Barboncito had made sure they had enough food to last the winter or, at least, until the soldiers left. But they ran short of water. So on a night brightly lit by the moon—and after the army had retired—the men formed a human chain down the face of Fortress Rock, locking arms from one to another. Along this chain they passed gourds hung on yucca rope. From a point 20 feet above Tsaile Creek—above the sleeping soldiers—they dropped the gourds into the creek and passed water back to the top of the butte.

It was an ingenious plan, but it was in vain. That January was not a snowy month but it was bitterly cold and, when the people began to suffer and Barboncito saw they would die of exposure, he had no alternative but to surrender and accept The Long Walk to the place they called *Hwééldi*—the Place of Great Suffering the army called Bosque Redondo.

According to the *Navajo Times*, the story of the standoff at *Tsélaa* is not well known, perhaps because it relies mostly on *Jiní*—a phrase sort of meaning *"Because I told you so."*

The National Park Service, which protects the canyon and the privacy of the Diné families who still choose to live there, does not mention the event, merely saying, "the use of this refuge continued into the 1860s." Moreover, the *Navajo Times* reports, most young people in the nearby town of Chinle would have a hard time finding Fortress Rock on a map. "But lest you doubt the story's veracity," Cindy Yurth writes for the paper, "Tsélaa itself holds the proof. If you know where to look, you can still see the treacherous ponderosa poles leaning against the cliffs, and the bulwarks of stone on top."

Jiní.

Edward Canby and Henry Hopkins Sibley
Best friends became enemies

Edward Canby and Henry Hopkins Sibley were best friends when they graduated from the United States Military Academy at West Point. Sibley graduated in 1838, Canby a year later. Both were commissioned second lieutenants—Sibley in the 2nd U.S. Dragoons and Canby in the 2nd U.S. Infantry. Both were intent on careers in the army. They were alleged to have married first cousins, but that proved to be rumor. We'll get to that intriguing part of the story later.

In April 1861, South Carolina secessionists fired on Union troops at Fort Sumter. A month later, Henry Sibley resigned his commission and joined the Confederacy. Canby remained an officer in the U.S. Army. Sibley's resignation might be understandable, considering he had been born in Natchitoches, Louisiana. But Canby's place of birth was Platt's Landing, Kentucky, so maybe it was just how deep into the South they had lived that determined how deep their sympathies were.

The two men now were lethal enemies—a sad commentary on two soldiers who had served together for more than 20 years.

Following their commissioning, both men fought together against Seminole Indians in Florida. They also fought in the West during Mexican-American War. Canby received brevet promotions to the rank of lieutenant colonel.

Sibley's career was more of a good news/bad news experience. The good news was, while on frontier duty in Texas following the war, he invented a personnel tent, modeled after Comanche tepees. Known as the Sibley Tent, it was used by both Union and Confederate armies throughout the Civil War, as well as by the United Kingdom up to World War I. He also devised a stove to heat the tent—one the army used into the early years of World War II.

The bad news of his career came after he feuded with Colonel Philip St. George Cooke, his regimental commander. In 1857, with the rank of captain, Sibley marched his company through winter to battle Mormons at Fort Bridger in Wyoming. He apparently disagreed with St. George Cooke's command, argued, and subsequently was court-martialed. Canby sat on the panel of judges and, whether that made a difference, Sibley was acquitted.

Both officers were assigned to New Mexico in 1860. Canby coordinated a campaign against the Navajo. Sibley was then subordinate to Colonel Canby. Both men were frustrated by the campaign, rarely sighting Navajo raiders. Usually they saw them only at a distance—never getting close to engage them.

Upon resigning his commission in 1861, Sibley traveled to Richmond, Virginia, where he persuaded Jefferson Davis, now president of the Confederacy, to adopt his plan to seize New Mexico Territory (today's states of New Mexico and Arizona) as well as Colorado and California. A successful campaign would open deep-water ports on the Pacific—the Confederacy was blockaded along the Atlantic by the Union navy—and access to gold fields in the Rocky Mountains, providing vital resources to prosecute the war.

Davis commissioned him a brigadier general and dispatched him to San Antonio to organize the 4th and 5th Texas Mounted Rifles, five companies of the 7th Texas Mounted Rifles, and six companies of the 2nd Texas Mounted Rifles. Known as Sibley's Brigade, the 2,500 mounted troops deployed in early 1862 to Mesilla, New Mexico, where John Baylor has defeated Union soldiers at Fort Filmore and established a base of operations. Sibley's plan was to march north through central New Mexico, capturing towns and supplies along the way, until he reached and engaged the army at Fort Union.

Fort Union was the central point of dispatch for the Quartermasters Corps, supplying Union installations throughout the Southwest. It was pivotal to Sibley's success.

But first, he had to take Fort Craig, about halfway between today's Truth or Consequences and Socorro. The 2,000 troops at Fort Craig were under the command of Edward Canby.

Confronting the Union army on February 19, 1862, Sibley demanded Canby surrender. Of course, he refused. The Confederate general may have considered a frontal assault foolhardy. One reason was Canby had had his men set out manikins—empty rifles under empty hats that looked like troopers at the ready. It was an empty gesture, but it was effective.

Instead, the Confederates, led by Colonel Tom Green, moved north a few miles to Valverde, where the Rio Grandé could be forded. Green was in command because Sibley was drunk, which he often was. We don't know if he was a alcoholic or suffering from unusual stress. In any case, his drinking left him incapacitated for command.

The ploy worked. Canby sent his army to meet the Confederates, and the battle was joined. The clash of armies surged back and forth across the river. At times, it seemed the Confederates would be defeated. Something had to be done to turn the tide of battle.

Colonel Green released his mounted Lancers, who had been waiting in an old river channel. They carried nine-foot-long pikes fixed with razor-sharp, 12-inch blades. The Mexicans had used the weapon effectively against Americans in California during the Mexican-American War. Now, the Texas Lancers popped up over the sandy embankment and charged the Union infantry. When the lancers had closed to within a hundred yards, Union soldiers began firing cannon loaded with antipersonnel canisters, mowing down the oncoming attackers. The skirmish lasted but a few minutes, leaving the ground littered in a tangle of horses and men. Green later said, the Lancers charge was one of the most gallant in the annals of battle—but they were no match for cannon at close range.

Kit Carson, serving under Canby, was ordered to take his First New Mexico Volunteers to defend Union artillery deployed along the east bank of the river. When the Texans attacked in force, the New Mexicans fired volley after volley into them. Carson continuously encouraged his men—most of whom were Mexican—*"Firme, Muchachos. Firme."*

To no avail, the Union lines to the left of the guns broke, and the Confederates overran them. Carson wanted to cross the river, believing he could still win the day. Good soldiers, however, follow orders, and he supervised an orderly retreat by his men, even with the Texans firing captured guns at them.

Other Union soldiers fled in disarray. As one Confederate later reported, "They ran like so many frightened mustangs."

With that, Canby determined he had risked too much and his fort was in jeopardy. He recalled his men and retreated. By nightfall of February 21, Confederates had lost 200 dead or wounded—the Union 263. Sibley again demanded surrender. Canby again refused, leaving the Confederate general no choice but to bury his dead and press northward.

Sibley's Brigade had won the field that bloody day, but they didn't capture the fort, and that proved a strategic failure that would become evident a month later at Glorieta Pass. Sibley continued toward his principal objective—Fort Union—capturing supplies in Albuquerque, most of which were burned by retreating Union troops, and occupying Santa Fe before attempting to dispel Union troops in Glorieta Pass, through which ran the Santa Fe Trail.

We'll pause here, in the war reporting, to contend with the intrigue swirling around the two soldier's wives. Henry Sibley had married Charlotte Kendall at Governor's Island, New York, in 1840. A year earlier, Edward Canby had taken Louisa Hawkins to wife at Crawfordsville, Indiana. Neither woman apparently knew each other, nor were they related, although stories floating like jetsam claimed they were first cousins. If that were true, Sibley and Canby would have been related by marriage.

The reason these rumors began was simply because of an act of compassion. Many of Sibley's wounded were left for treatment in Santa Fe, while his army moved into Glorieta Pass. The kindness toward these men by Louisa Canby, who was living in Santa Fe, stimulated a whispering campaign the Kentucky-born officer's wife was actually the Louisiana general's sister. Then they naturally morphed into other stories, ending with the two women being cousins and the combatants being brothers-in-law.

The battle of Glorieta Pass is too complex story to relate here. Suffice it to say, during the first day of fighting, Confederates held their own and were positioned to overrun Union forces deployed at Pigeon's Ranch. Pigeon had built a wall across the valley floor, forcing travelers to use his toll bridge over Glorieta Creek.

Fearing defeat, Colonel John Slough, commanding the Union troops, dispatched Major John Chivington to climb to the ridge line of the pass and drop in behind Sibley's men. Instead he got lost. When he located the Confederates, he did not find the troopers. What he found was Sibley's wagon train of supplies, which he burned. Without supplies, the Confederate general had no choice but to retreat, fighting for the life of his brigade until he withdrew completely from New Mexico. The Confederates never returned.

Following the war, Sibley was dispatched as military adviser to Ima'l Pasha, the *Khedive* (viceroy) of Egypt, overseeing construction of coastal fortifications. Because of his alcoholism, he was dismissed from illness and disability. He died in poverty and was buried in Fredericksburg, Virginia.

Canby, meanwhile, accepted several assignments in the South during Reconstruction. In 1872, he was posted to command the Pacific Northwest, attempting to make peace with the Modoc. He had conflicting orders from Washington—make peace or make war? Thinking they were deceived, the Modoc swore to kill Canby. When Canby explained he had no authority to promise the Modoc their own country, one of the warriors shot him twice in the head and cut his throat. Canby became the only general to be killed in the Indian Wars. His body was returned for interment in Indianapolis, Indiana.

We get to choose our friends. We don't always get to determined the circumstances under which we live. Edward Canby and Henry Sibley had the misfortune to be born at what has to have been the worst time ever for Americans to have tried to be *best friends forever.*

Albert Pfeiffer — Army Captain
He had a love/hate relationship with Indians

What does it take to turn a man from friend and defendant of the Ute people to a vengeful hater of all Indians?

Albert Pfeiffer's story is a living example of the love/hate relationship many Anglos in the West had toward Indians.

Born in Germany, Albert Hinrich Pfeiffer emigrated to the United States in 1844. He was 22 years old when the lure of the West compelled him to cross the plains from St. Louis to Santa Fe.

There, he became a clerk in a mercantile owned by Joseph Hersch. Later he moved to Abiquiu, where he married Antonia, daughter of an influential Mexican family. When a trading post opened in Abiquiu, Pfeiffer was chosen as the subagent for the Ute tribe, a post that required patience and the ability of negotiate with people of a totally different culture.

In October 1859, trouble had broken out between settlers and the Ute, a not uncommon occurrence considering how many times Anglos and Mexicans simply usurped Indian lands because they could. Kit Carson discussed with Pfeiffer the difficulties with the Tabegauche Utes. He wrote to James Collins, superintendent of Indian affairs in New Mexico and his superior, "Give to me and Pfeiffer authority to give good and peaceable talks." With that authority, they engaged in negotiations with the Utes. The outcome was favorable, creating not only peaceful relations but also a lifelong friendship with Ute Chief Ouray.

That brings us to the Civil War. When hostilities broke out in the East, Pfeiffer enlisted with the New Mexico Volunteers, serving under Kit Carson. In July 1861, John Baylor, who led a contingent of Confederate Texas Volunteers, attacked and captured Mesilla. He established his headquarters there and declared the southern half of New Mexico Territory to be the Confederate state of Arizona.

On his heels came General Henry Hopkins Sibley. His mission was to capture Fort Union with its quartermaster's base of supply for the entire Southwest. That would give the Confederates access to Pacific deep water ports and the gold fields of Colorado. Confederate and Union troops met at Fort Craig in March 1862.

The two armies faced off in the village of Valverde seven miles north of the fort. Pfeiffer was riding with Carson and the First New Mexico Volunteers. Union Colonel Edward Canby sent the Volunteers to the east bank of the Rio Grandé to prevent the Texans from attacking the fort while Union soldiers battled at Valverde. The contest ended in a draw. The Confederates failed to capture the fort. The Union failed to defeat the Texans and drive them out of New Mexico.

In 1863, Pfeiffer was promoted to captain and given command of Fort McRae, three miles east of the Rio Grandé near Palomas (today's Truth or Consequence). The fort's mission was to protect settlers and travelers from bandits and Apache raiders.

In a quiet moment, when the Mescalero and Chiricahua were not raiding, Pfeiffer, who suffered from rheumatism, went to soak in the warm mineral springs bubbling out of the ground at Palomas. He took his wife, Antonia, their adopted daughter, Maria, and Mrs. Mercado, their servant woman, along with a contingent of soldiers acting as guards. You'd think a man could enjoy a soak in peace?

Without warning, a band of Mescalero attacked, quickly killing several of the guards and scattering the rest. The Apache captured Pfeiffer's wife, daughter, and servant. Pfeiffer scrambled into nearby rocks to fire back. In the fray, he was shot with an arrow that protruded through his chest just below his heart. Nearly naked and wounded, he defended himself for several hours.

When the Mescalero broke off the battle and left, Pfeiffer—severely sunburnt and weak from his wound—had no alternative but to hike back to the fort. There, the army surgeon removed the arrow, and Pfeiffer was at the point for death for nearly two months. Yet he survived.

Troops rode out to find his wife, daughter, and servant. When the army finally caught up with the Apaches, they now considered their captives encumbrances and killed them.

As retold in newspapers for nearly 20 years, Pfeiffer's plight became even more dire, while his survival became even more heroic.

Meanwhile, the captain went on to become a vengeful Indian fighter.

He had come to hate the Dinè and soon learned why these people were called Navajo—a pejorative used by Puebloans. It meant ancient enemy and was used so frequently it has become the common name by which the Dinè are known.

To prevent war between the Utes and Navajo over hot springs in southern Colorado, waters the Utes claimed to have possessed for generations, Pfeiffer suggested a deal. Both tribes agreed each would offer only one man using a Bowie knife to battle the other to the death. The winner would take possession of the springs. The other would leave peacefully.

The Navajo put up their biggest, seasoned warrior. Pfeiffer so hated the Dinè, he volunteered to do the battle. By now, he was a middle age man—in his forties—and only about five and a half feet tall. Part of the deal required the men to face off nude. It must have been a sight. The young, muscular bronze-skin Dinè surely laughed at the prospect of fighting the old white man—until Pfeiffer disrobed. Naked, Pfeiffer presented a grizzled-hair-covered chest and back through which shown the glistening tissue of his many battle scars. The Navajo was so intimidated, Pfeiffer easily defeated him. So the Utes continued their possession of the hot springs.

Then, Pfeiffer was assigned by General James Carleton, commander of Fort Sumner, to join Kit Carson in rounding up the Navajo in their homeland and marching them to Bosque Redondo, a resettlement camp near the fort.

In January 1864, Carson and Pfeiffer left Fort Defiance with 375 troopers for Canyon de Chelly, a Dinè stronghold. More than a foot of snow covered the ground and temperatures were well below zero. A reporter embedded with the troops wrote, "The frost was so intense, hardy resolute men groaned from the pain of it."

Carson split his command. He entered the west end of Canyon de Chelly, sending Pfeiffer with Company H to the east end. The captain was only to reconnoiter but, impatient to engage the Dinè, he forged into the canyon. Pfeiffer had entered what today is called Canyon del Muerto, which adjoins the main canyon. The army was unaware of the side canyon at the time.

From canyon walls from 600 to 1,000 feet high, the Dinè fired arrows and threw rocks at the troop below. In his report, Pfeiffer wrote, "Indians on both sides of the Canyon, whooping, yelling, and cursing, firing shots and throwing rocks down upon my command. Killed two buck Indians in the encounter and one squaw, who obstinately persisted in throwing rocks and pieces of wood."

Where Canyon del Muerto meets Canyon de Chelly, there is a pinnacle, today called Fortress Rock. On top were 300 Dinè. (You can read the story of Chief Barboncito and the standoff at Fortress Rock elsewhere in this book.)

"Here the Navajos sought refuge when pursued by the invading force," Pfeiffer continued in his report, "whether of neighboring tribes or of the arms of the government, and here they were enabled to jump about on the ledges like mountain cats, hallooing at me, swearing and cursing and threatening vengeance on my command."

Fortress Rock stands 700 feet tall, a height so great neither the Dinè nor the soldiers could do much harm to each other.

When Carson finally discovered Pfeiffer's location, the troops of Company H had killed three Dinè and captured 19. The army lay siege to the pinnacle and waited while the cold of winter and dwindling food supplies caused the Dinè finally to surrender.

The Canyon de Chelly campaign broke the Dinè's resistance and convinced them to begin what came to be known as The Long Walk from their beloved Dinétah to the horror of Bosque Redondo, the place they call *Hwééldi* or the place of suffering.

Pfeiffer's encounters with Indians and his bravery continued. Six months later, in June 1864, he was wounded again in a fight with Apaches in northern Arizona. The local Colorado newspaper noted, "There is hardly room for a fresh cut or bullet hole in his body."

Despite all of his battles and wounds, Albert Pfeiffer — worn out and covered with scars — died in his bed at age 57. That he did not die among cactus and rocks in some lonely place was a miracle in itself, wrote author and historian Jim Perkins.

Cathay Williams
Buffalo Soldier in disguise

"I wanted to make my own living and not be dependent on relations or friends."

That's what Cathay Williams said when explaining her adventure as a Buffalo Soldier.

Williams was born a slave, belonging to William Johnson, a wealthy farmer who settled in Jefferson City, Missouri. Williams explained, "My father was a freeman, but my mother belonged to Master Johnson."

Shortly after the outbreak of the Civil War, Union soldiers took control of the territory and rounded up slaves, which they called contraband. They were, after all, property of plantation owners, no different than horses, wagons, and cotton bales. Said Williams, "The soldiers came to Jefferson City. They took me and other colored folk with them to Little Rock. I did not want to go."

Most of the men were pressed into service. Apparently it didn't take too much "pressing," as 186,000 African-Americans fought on the Union side.

Williams, than 17 years old, enlisted as a cook for the 8th Indiana Volunteer Infantry Regiment, commanded by William Plummer Benton. "He wanted me to cook for the officers," Williams said, "but I had always been a house girl and did not know how to cook." She was taught.

"I was with the army at the battle of Pea Ridge. Afterwards we moved over various portions of Arkansas and Louisiana. I saw soldiers burn lots of cotton and was at Shreveport when rebel gunboats were captured and burned on Red River. We afterwards went to New Orleans, then by way of the Gulf to Savannah, Georgia, then to Macon and other places in the South. Finally, I was sent to Washington City and, at the time, General Sheridan made his raids in the Shenandoah valley, I was cook and washwoman for his staff."

At the close of the Civil War, the U.S. government found itself with more than 180,000 African-Americans still enlisted as soldiers. Southerners and eastern populations did not want to see armed, black men in their communities. Whites also did not want the African-Americans' competition for the limited number of jobs. To ameliorate the situation, Congress created two regiments of cavalry and six infantry regiments for African-Americans. They would serve on the western frontier.

These men came to be called Buffalo Soldiers, a name attributed to them by the Navajo, Apache, Comanche, and other tribes. Some said, because of their black skin and hair, they resembled the buffalo. Others said it was because of their fortitude, their willingness—like the buffalo—to stand and fight. There are stories of Buffalo Soldiers fighting Indians, long after their white counterparts had retreated, firing their rifles until the barrels got to hot to hold. It was this fortitude the native people admired.

Mustered out of the army, Williams faced an even more formidable challenge—being free yet unemployed. She had to wonder how she would provide for herself.

On November 15, 1866, she enlisted for a three-year tour of duty in the army, along with a male cousin and a best friend, the only other people who would know she was female. Williams knew women were prohibited from serving in the military, but she may have heard stories about women passing themselves off as men to fight and serve. So, she changed her name to William Cathay and informed her recruiting officer she was a 22-year-old cook. He described her as five-foot, nine-inches tall, with black eyes, black hair, and black complexion.

An Army surgeon examined her and determined she was fit for duty. It's apparent the post-Civil War enlistment process did not include a physical or presentation of any legal documents. She was a black woman, so the recruiter probably rightly reasoned she had been a slave, now freed, but who would not likely have a birth certificate. He assumed she was who she claimed to be.

"The regiment I joined wore the Zouave uniform and only two persons, a cousin and a particular friend, members of the regiment, knew I was a woman. They never 'blowed' on me," she said.

The Zouave uniform may have unwittingly assisted her in her disguise. It was based on the elite Zouave battalion of the French army—the

French always making a fashion statement. The uniform featured baggy, red knee-britches, loose-fitting, red blouse, vest, sash, and a distinctive, embroidered blue jacket. The uniform included a red fez with a gold tassel. The French had modeled its Zouave uniform after the native dress of former Algerian opponents, whose fearless tactics during the colonial war of the 1830s they admired.

It's likely the men—and woman—who wore the Zouave uniform thought of themselves as better dressed than those in the standard blue trousers and dark blue blouse of other army regiments.

During her enlistment, Williams was plagued with illness. She contracted smallpox and was hospitalized—but was able to maintain her disguise. She recovered well enough to rejoin her unit, then posted in New Mexico.

Duty in New Mexico was harsh for everyone, but especially for the Buffalo Soldiers. White soldiers got the best accommodations, the best food, and even the best mounts. Patrols in the desert were long and dangerous both from native people defending their homelands and natural phenomenon, like snakes and lightning.

"I carried my musket and did guard and other duties while in the army," Williams said, "but finally I got tired and wanted to get off. I played sick, complained of pains in my side, and rheumatism in my knees." She also suffered from neuralgia and diabetes and had had toes amputated from frostbite. She could walk only with a crutch.

During her three-year tour, she was hospitalized at least five times before the post surgeon discovered she was a woman. What took so long? She may not have been required to fully undress or maybe she simply made excuses not to reveal her gender. However, on October 14, 1868, the surgeon informed Captain Charles Clarke, post commander, and, as Williams said, "I got my discharge."

Despite her service and illness, Cathay Williams was denied a pension. One history reports, "Having served as a man should not have been a factor and she should have received the pension, like white women Deborah Sampson, Margaret Corbin and Mary Hays McCauley (who fought as men in the Revolutionary War) did. Cathay Williams had no one to fight for her pension rights and, therefore, got nothing."

That's not entirely correct. Cathay Williams is remembered in history as the only woman to serve in the army as a Buffalo Soldier as well as the only documented black woman known to have served when enlisting women was prohibited.

Roy Bean — the "Hanging" Judge
It takes a scoundrel to know a scoundrel

Most everyone has heard of Judge Roy Bean, who called himself *All the law west of the Pecos*. Judge Bean tried many a notorious scoundrel, but — as the saying goes — "It takes one to know one," and Roy Bean was as much a scoundrel as the men who came before him.

Born in Kentucky in 1825, the youngest of five, Roy left home at age 16 to find work in New Orleans. What he found was trouble, causing him to flee to San Antonio, Texas, to join his brother, Sam. We are told, Sam apparently was the son who did everything right. Roy was the son who did everything wrong. That about sums up Roy Bean's life.

In 1848, the two brothers had a trading post in Chihuahua. Roy killed a Mexican desperado, who had threatened to kill a *gringo*. To escape a murder charge by Mexican authorities, Roy dragged his brother with him first to Sonora and, by 1849, to San Diego, California.

Considered a handsome lad by the ladies, Roy competed for the attentions of the local women. But the competition took a turn for the worse when it involved a pistol-shooting match on horseback between Bean and a Scotsman named Collins. Bean was left to choose the targets. He decided they'd shoot at each other and dueled with pistols in February 1852, ending with Collins being shot in his right arm. Both men were arrested and charged with assault with intent to murder. In the two months he was in jail, Bean received many gifts of flowers, food, wine, and cigars from female admirers. His final gift while incarcerated was a knife encased in tamales, which Bean used to dig through the cell wall and escape.

Two years later, Bean courted a woman who was kidnapped and forced to marry a Mexican officer. Bean challenged him to a duel and killed him. Six of the dead man's friends put Bean on a horse, tied a noose around his neck, and left him to hang. However, the horse did not bolt and, after the men left, the bride, who had been hiding behind a tree, cut the rope to set him free. Bean was left with a scar on his neck from the rope.

It seemed a good time to leave California. Roy migrated to New Mexico to live once again with Sam, who had been elected the first sheriff of Doña Ana County. The two brothers operated a store and saloon in Pino Alto, advertising good liquor and a fine billiard table to attract local miners. Apparently, Apache depredations proved too much, and the brothers moved to Mesilla. There they opened a saloon in the building that today houses El Patio Cantina on Calle de Parìan, across from the plaza. Being an upstanding citizen and sheriff, Sam Bean kept fellow citizens cash and valuables, along with his own money, in his safe. Just how safe the safe was remains to be seen.

In 1861, Texas Confederates invaded and occupied Mesilla, leading to two Civil War battles — one at Valverde and the other at Glorieta Pass. The two battles were fought to a draw and, except for Union soldiers locating and burning the Confederate wagon train, with its supplies, the Confederates might have won. Instead, they retreated along the Rio Grandé and back into Texas. (See the story in this book about Edward Canby and Henry Hopkins Sibley and the Battle of Valverde.)

While Sam apparently was away from the saloon on business, Roy opened and emptied the safe, joining the retiring defeated Confederate army. For the remainder of the war, he ran blockades, hauling cotton to and supplies from British ships off Matamoros.

Following the Civil War, Roy Bean made his way in San Antonio. For the 20 years, he tried one business after another. He ran a firewood business, cutting his neighbor's trees for timber. He attempted to run a dairy but was caught watering down the milk. He also worked as a butcher, rendering into steaks and chops cattle rustled from area ranchers.

While engaged in these questionable enterprises, Bean married Virginia Chavez. It was 1866. Bean was 45 years old; Virginia was 18. Within a year of being married, he was arrested for aggravated assault and threatening his wife's life. Despite their troubles, Roy and Virginia produced four children.

They lived in Beanville, a poverty-stricken slum adjoining San Antonio. In the late 1870s, Bean operated a saloon, serving workers of the expanding railroad. He was considered to be such an unscrupulous character, one store owner in town was so anxious to have him out of town, he bought all of Roy's possessions for $900 so he could leave. Indeed, he left San Antonio, abandoning his wife and four children.

By the spring of 1882, Bean had established a small saloon near the Pecos River in a tent city he named Vinegaroon, after the common arachnid called a giant whip scorpion, which has no venom glands but sprays acid in its defense. With his ready cash, he purchased supplies and ten 55-gallon barrels of whiskey to sell.

Within 20 miles of the tent city were 8,000 railroad workers. The nearest court was 200 miles away at Fort Stockton, and there was little means to stop illegal activity. A Texas Ranger requested local law jurisdiction be set up in Vinegaroon and, on August 2, 1882, Roy Bean was appointed justice of the peace for the new Precinct 6 in Pecos County.

One of his first acts was to "shoot up the saloon shack of a Jewish competitor." Bean then turned his tent saloon into a part-time courtroom and began calling himself the "Law West of the Pecos." As judge, Bean relied on a single law book, the 1879 edition of the *Revised Statutes of Texas*. When newer law books showed up, he used them as kindling.

Bean was known for his unusual rulings. In one case, an Irishman named Paddy O'Rourke shot a Chinese laborer. A mob of angry Irishmen surrounded the courtroom and threatened to lynch Bean if O'Rourke was not freed. After looking through his law book, Bean ruled "homicide was the killing of a human being." However, he could find no law against killing a Chinaman. The case was dismissed. O'Rourke walked free.

Bean moved west, keeping pace with the railroad and walking once again into trouble. Unable to attract customers in Strawbridge, because a competitor had laced Bean's whiskey with kerosene, he moved to Eagle's

Nest and renamed it Langtry, after actress Lillie Langtry, the love of his life, though it's unlikely he ever actually met her.

The owner of the land on which Bean settled already ran a saloon. He sold land to the railroad on the condition no land be leased to Roy. Paddy O'Rourke, the man whose life he had saved, advised Bean to use the railroad right-of-way, not covered in the contract. For the next 20 years, he squatted on land for which he had no legal right and built a saloon he named The Jersey Lillie, after actress Langtry.

Known as the "hanging judge," Beam tried only two men for capital offense. One was hanged, the other escaped. Mostly, since he did not have a jail, he settled cases by fine. Instead of sending the state the fines, which happened to be to the exact amount the accused had, he pocketed it. In cases involving stolen horses, thieves were fined and allowed to go if they returned the animals.

Bean won re-election as justice of the peace in 1884 but was defeated two years later. In 1887, the commissioner's court created a new precinct in the county and appointed Bean to be the justice of the peace. He continued in office until he was defeated in 1896. Yet, even after that defeat, he refused to surrender his seal and law book and continued to try all cases.

The year he lost the election he had an "even better idea." He organized a world championship boxing title bout between Bob Fitzsimmons and Peter Mather. The ring was built on an island in the middle of the Rio Grandé because neither Texas or Mexico condoned boxing matches. Within a minute and a half of the first round, Fitzsimmons knocked Mather out. Not only did Bean earn a sizable sum of money from the fight, but his fame also spread throughout the country.

Now, you might think Roy Bean was a scoundrel and once a scoundrel always a scoundrel, but he seemed to have a soft side. He spent much of his profits helping the poor in the area and always made sure the schoolhouse had firewood for winter.

After a bout of heavy drinking, Roy Bean died in his sleep in 1903. A legend of the Old West had finally joined so many others.

"Uncle Dick" Wootton and Raymond Morley
Conquerors of Raton Pass

When you cruise Interstate 25 between Trinidad, Colorado, and Raton, New Mexico, you're not likely to think about how hard it was for the first people to traverse these mountains. Earliest travelers followed animal trails. Later, people struggled over the pass in wagons. The two men of this story, "Uncle Dick" Wootton and Raymond Morley, both made it easier—the first by graded toll road, the other by railroad.

Richens Lacy Wootton, "Uncle Dick" by his friends, was 19 years old when he took a job wrangling wagons across the Santa Fe Trail for Bent, St. Vrain and Company. The West seduced him just like a dancing girl in a Denver saloon. There was nothing for him back east, except his uncle's cotton plantation in Mississippi, a venture fraught with the vicissitudes of nature: too much rain, too little rain, weevils, rot, and sundry other common plagues—not to mention the heat and bugs everyone endured just to harvest the fluffy bolls.

The West wrapped its arms around him, embraced him, showed him freedom he could not imagine any more than the slaves picking for his uncle near Natchez

Wootton embarked Independence, Missouri, in 1836, driving a wagon loaded with merchandise for Bent's Fort in southeast Colorado. He'd never seen anything to compare with what was before him. The wagon did 12 miles a day, from the rising to the setting of the sun. He often felt they'd not moved at all; the rolling grasslands seemed unchanged. But he paid attention. He listened, and he watched. The wagon master was only too eager to teach an impressionable, willing young man. Before he reached the fort, Wootton could distinguish features indistinguishable to others, locate seeps and springs from subtle gradation of green, and even gage distances. He learned the rudiments of tracking, and he learned to shoot.

For years thereafter, he used Bent's Fort as his base of operations, living as a mountain man, trapper, and hunter. But now he needed to support his wife and children. By the time he died at age 77, he had out-lived five wives and 17 of his 20 children.

Earning a living was essential but had become increasingly more difficult. The beaver had been trapped out, and the bison were rapidly disappearing from the plains, indiscriminately slaughtered by men seeking only the buffalo's tongue and hide. The remainder of the animal Plains Indians had used from snout to tail was left to rot. "Uncle Dick" needed a new vocation.

In 1866, the Civil War was over. Settlers were streaming west to find new lives. Wootton came to Trinidad, Colorado, and obtained permission from the territorial governments of both Colorado and New Mexico to build a toll road over Raton Pass.

Susan Magoffin, in her diary, turned book, *Down the Santa Fe Trail and Into Mexico*, told of the hardship on animals, wagons, and people attempting to cross the trackless Sangre de Cristo Mountains to obtain Santa Fe. The most accessible pass was nearly 8,000 feet above sea level, more than 3,000 feet above the surrounding plains.

Wootton set out to build a road easier on everyone. Most people he approached to work on his project declined. They thought the work too hard. Instead, he enlisted members of the Ute tribe, under Chief Connia-che, to help him construct 27 miles over the hardest part of the pass.

Said Wootton, "There were hillsides to cut down, rocks to blast and remove, and bridges to build by the score. But I built the road and made it a good one."

He erected a tollgate in front of his house, charging $1.50 for a wagon or buggy to use the road — 25 cents for a horseman. For as long as Wootton owned the road, he never charged the Indians toll. Because of their help, they always got a free pass.

During crossings, stagecoaches stopped at his home to pay the toll. To supplement his income, Wootton and his wife served passengers a hot meal. He had found a new occupation, one that didn't take him away from his family for months at a time, one that allowed him to sit on the porch, wait for patrons to call, and count his coin.

In the 1840s, Cyrus Holliday worked on a railroad back east. He wanted his own line. When he had accumulated $20,000—more than $500,000 in today's currency—he had enough to start. Unfortunately, the Civil War intervened. When it ended, Holliday was ready to start in Lawrence, Kansas, and build all the way to California. He called his railroad the Atchinson, Topeka and Santa Fe. His goal was to build through New Mexico Territory and on west. First, he had to conquer Raton Pass.

Holliday offered Uncle Dick Wootton $50,000 for his toll road. Wooton turned him down, but he liked these Santa Fe railroad men—much more than he liked J.A. McMurtrie, who was chief engineer for the Denver and Rio Grande railroad—a man he disliked with a vengeance. When Wootton learned the Denver and Rio Grande was competing with the Santa Fe to build over Raton Pass, he changed his mind. He sold the right away to Albert Robinson, the Santa Fe's chief engineer, for a dollar—plus a monthly stipend and grocery money for his wife for the rest of her life.

Now, the law in those days stated the company who first began construction won the right away to the railroad line. In 1877, Robinson discretely sent Raymond Morley, his location engineer, to survey the pass.

Ray Morley had already made a name for himself with the Santa Fe. He had been instrumental in laying out the rail line across the plains. Now his skills were needed for the daunting task of conquering Raton Pass.

Agnes Morley Cleaveland, his daughter, in her book *No Life For a Lady*, writes, "There is extant enough historical data to establish the fact his engineering ability amounted to genius." He would need every ounce of that genius to succeed.

Morley dressed in shepherd's clothing and masqueraded as a shepherd while he surveyed and measured the route the railroad would have to take. McMurtrie never discovered the "wolf in sheep's clothing," sitting around a campfire—ostensibly herding ewes and lambs—was seriously occupied securing the pass for the Santa Fe.

McMurtrie was perhaps overconfident. Moreover, he was greedy. Trinidad wanted a railroad to maintain its location as a major route of travel. McMurtrie, however, wanted to cash in on the real estate he owned at his proposed townsite of El Moro. He stopped building his railroad four miles from Trinidad. The town's people were outraged.

The Denver and Rio Grande had surveyed the pass in 1876 but had failed to file a plat and profile the route. McMurtrie believed he had no rival nor did he believe the Santa Fe could assemble a crew in time to beat him to the pass.

Morley and McMurtrie were both on the train from Pueblo to take possession of Raton Pass. Morley stayed hidden behind his hat and perhaps newspaper. When the train reached the end of the line, Morley gave up his bed for a horse and rode throughout the night to Wootton's house.

With the old mountain man's help, Morley—and Robinson who had also arrived—secured the crew they needed—furious men from Trinidad. By the time the unsuspecting McMurtrie arrived, the Santa Fe crew was already staking out the only route to northern New Mexico. They had established possession by the right of prior construction.

By 1878, the Santa Fe crew finishing cutting a 2,000-foot-long tunnel in the mountains to make it feasible for trains to pass. Still, they were forced to deal with grades reaching as high a 3.5 % at the top of the pass and 4% in some places on the Colorado side.

Having conquered Raton Pass and laid track over the Santa Fe Trail through Glorieta Pass to Santa Fe, Morley went on to other challenges. The need for his skills were unabated, and he was sent to build the first railroad in Mexico, connecting Guaymas to Nogales, Arizona.

Cleaveland remembers riding with her father on the cowcatcher of the work train, chugging along at 20 miles an hour. "To me it was hurtling through space with a comet's speed," she wrote. "With my father's arms about me, making everything safe and right ... I felt an exalted sense of dominion."

If the Santa Fe hadn't already, this railroad project launched Morley upon a career of assured achievement and honor. Before the Guaymas-Nogales line had been completed, he had already been engaged to build a more important line, the Mexican Central, with its terminus in Mexico City. He was never to see the completion of this line.

Seated in a two-person hack, he asked the driver to move the rifle resting across the back of the seat, saying he didn't like the weapon pointed at him. The driver laughed and jerked the reins free from the gunstock around which they had become entangled. The gun accidentally discharged, killing Morley, and radically changing the lives of his widow, son, and daughter. As Cleaveland wrote, "The explosion brought the firmament crashing down upon a little family's head."

The next time you cruise the Interstate over Raton Pass, take a moment to reflect on the two men who made your journey possible.

Juan Maria Agostini-Justiniani
El Ermitaño de La Cueva

L a Cueva is the name given to an outcrop of volcanic tuff at the base of the Organ Mountains east of Las Cruces. It runs northwest to southeast about a quarter mile, is maybe a hundred to so yards thick, and about 300 feet at its highest point. It's a popular hangout for hikers and rock climbers.

But its name, *La Cueva*, says it's a cave, not a rough and tumble chunk of rock.

On the southeast corner of the outcrop, there is indeed a cave, a rock shelter occupied by Paleo-Indians as far back as 5,000 BCE. Later peoples, namely the Jornada Mogollon and, more recently, the Apache used the shelter.

Archaeological studies and excavations have produced about 100,000 artifacts from the cave. Pieces of baskets and yucca fiber sandals, stone tools, and animal bones: rabbit, deer, antelope, and bighorn sheep. From what has been found, archaeologists conclude everyone who used the cave spent most of their time outside and retreated to its interior only in times of bad weather.

Everyone. Except one. A man who came to be know as *El Ermitaño de La Cueva* — The Hermit of La Cueva.

The hermit was Juan Maria Agostini-Justiniani, born to Italian nobles in 1800. He allegedly studied to be a priest but he could not accede to his sacred vows. Instead, he abandoned the priesthood and spent many years wandering Europe, South America, Mexico, and Cuba, accumulating substantial knowledge of botany and the healing powers of plants. Along the way, he became a skilled healer.

By his sixty-second year, Agostini walked with the wagon train of Eugenio Romero from Kansas City to Las Vegas, New Mexico. For awhile, he lived in Romeroville, about ten miles south, but migrated to a mountain northwest of the village, a 10,000-foot mountain called *Cerro Tecolote*, where he lived in solitude. There he carved crucifixes and religious emblems which he traded for food. To this day, it's still called "Hermit's Peak" and not Owl Mountain.

In 1867, he accompanied the wagon train of Don Ramon Gonzales to Mesilla to find Colonel Albert J. Fountain and discuss a legal matter. Fountain was one of the best known lawyers in the territory at the time. His legal issue resolved, Agostini walked to San Antonio, Texas, then back to a cave near Ciudad Juarez, and finally to Mesilla.

In 1869, he often visited the Barela family on the plaza and sometimes preached in their home. He also applied his healing powers to people far and wide, but the notoriety may have been too much for the introspective man.

One day, he announced his plans to trek 20 miles across the desert to the cave in the outcrop of rock at the base of the Organ Mountains, intent of making his home there. He would not be dissuaded and followed through with his plans. Believers would make their way to the mysterious healer at the cave, where they found cures for their ailments, cures concocted from the herbs and flowers he gathered from the desert outside his haven.

Genuinely concerned for his safety, his friends had warned him of the dangers of staying in the cave alone. To appease them, he told them, "I shall make a fire in front of my cave every Friday evening while I shall be alive. If the fire ever fails to appear, it will be because I have been killed."

On a Friday in the spring of 1869, Antonio Garcia failed to see the fire lighting the mouth of the cave. Garcia was aware of Agostini's healing powers and often transported sick people to *El Ermitaño* to be healed. That night, Garcia led a posse to the mountains, only to find Agostini lying facedown, dead on the floor of La Cueva. He lay on a large crucifix he apparently had held in his hands. He was wearing a penitential girdle of metal spikes. A knife protruded from his back.

El Ermitaño was buried in the Mesilla Cemetery. His epitaph is in Spanish. It says, "John Mary Justiniani, Hermit of the Old and New World. He died the 17th of April, 1869, at 69 years and 49 years as a hermit."

His murderer was never found nor has anyone ever figured out why anyone would have wanted him dead. Agostini-Justiniani's death remains one of New Mexico's most infamous, unsolved murders to this very day.

There are, incidentally, stories of a ghost igniting a phantom fire-light in front of La Cueva on rare moonless nights. With the gate to the Dripping Springs Recreational Area closed at sunset by the Bureau of Land Management rangers, it would be hard to check out the story. However, if you parked outside the gate and illegally walked in, you could sit in the silent isolation in front of La Cueva and wait. But, then ... if you saw a fire, would you want to meet who lit it?

Elfego Baca — Deputy Sheriff
The infamous "Frisco War"

"**I** will show Texans there is at least one Mexican who is not afraid of an American cowboy."

So said Elfego Baca at the start of what came to be called the "Frisco War."

In the last half of the 19th century, New Mexico was a vast territory in which law enforcement was not much more than empty words — as empty as the desert is of trees. This may be the principal reason Congress rejected New Mexicans' application for statehood 14 times — the first in 1850 because of racial issues but the others because people back east thought the territory was lawless and, anyway, filled with just Mexicans and Indians, most of whom were Catholic and thus un-American.

Socorro County, where this event took place, stretched 750 miles from Texas to California, although it was only about 50 miles wide, north to south. It was just too much territory for the sheriff to provide law enforcement, so Anglo cowboys demeaned and bullied people of Mexican descent pretty much at will. Some still do to this day.

In 1884, Elfego Baca was 19 years old. He acquired some guns and became a deputy sheriff in Socorro County. Some say he was appointed. Others say he purchased his badge, or he may just have declared himself a deputy, liking the swagger that went with the job. His ascendency to peace officer was not uncommon. Honest men and even men who had been outlaws — men with "grit" — often took on the job of controlling those who lived for themselves and not the community.

In any event, in October of that year, Frisco Deputy Sheriff Pedro Sarracino rode to Socorro for help. Seven drunk cowboys with the outfit of cattleman John Slaughter had brutally tortured a man known as El Burro. When his friend, Epitacia Martinez, came to his aid, the cowboys bound him and used him for target practice. Both men survived.

Frisco — today's Reserve, New Mexico — was a stop along the stock driveway ending at the railhead in Magdalena. It was a hard, three-day ride from Socorro. When Baca arrived in Frisco, he saw Charlie McCarty, one of Slaughter's cowboys, butting a man on the head and firing several rounds to terrorize him. He was advised by the justice of the peace to stand back because Slaughter had a 150 cowboys on his payroll — and they all seemed to be in Frisco. There seemed to be nothing the locals could do.

But Baca was fearless — or perhaps foolish. He grabbed McCarty from Bill Milligan's saloon and hauled the drunken man off to jail, confiscating his guns.

Soon a bunch of the Slaughter outfit pulled up in front of the jail. Foreman Young Parham called the deputy outside and demanded McCarty be handed over to him. Baca refused. When Parham put his hand on the butt of his Colt, Baca thought he was pulling on him. The lawman drew his gun and shot Parham's horse. He'd been aiming for the foreman's chest. The terrified horse reared, dumped Parham to the ground, and then fell on him, crushing him to death.

Baca continued firing wildly, hitting another cowboy in the knee. Slaughter's men fled.

Justice of the Peace Ted White conducted a hearing of the incident. Baca brought McCarty to court. Milligan and some of Slaughter's men were also present. Milligan declined to press charges. No one in his bar had been hurt, and there was no significant damage. White fined McCarty for disorderly conduct and released him.

An incensed Baca left the court, still in possession of McCarty's pistols. When the Slaughter boys demanded he return the cowboy's guns, Baca left town and took refuge in a *jacal* behind the home of Geronimo Armijo. A *jacal* is a shack made by sticking slabs of wood vertically in the ground and dripping adobe slip in the cracks. It's roofed over with *vigas, latillas*, brush, and dirt. Armijo's *jacal* was partially dug out, its floor 18 inches below grade.

Judge White sent Bert Hearne, a popular rancher from Spur Lake Ranch, to bring Baca in for questioning in the death of Parham. The deputy refused to give himself up. Hearne kicked in the door and ordered Baca to come out with his hands up. Baca answered with two shots. One struck Hearne in the gut and killed him.

Now, Hearne was liked by everyone in Frisco, so the Slaughter cowboys and others—a disputed number of 40 to 80 men—took the law in their own hands. For more than a day—some say 33 hours—the cowboys plastered the *jacal* with more than 1,000 rounds. Like enraged hornets, bullets assailed the mud and timber shack. Legend has it they fired more than 4,000 rounds, but there's little evidence to confirm that. After attempting to approach the *jacal* with an iron-stove door for a shield, one attacker fell back with his scalp neatly creased by a bullet.

A shootout on this scale, like a hanging, was the best entertainment Frisco had had in awhile. Villagers climbed to hilltops—though carefully out of range—to watch. One can image cheers, and arguments, and even betting on the outcome.

As daylight faded, the cowboys were able to toss flaming, kerosene-soaked rags onto the roof of the *jacal*. Under the combined assault of lead and fire, one wall and a portion of the roof collapsed on its sole occupant. When the cowboys ran out of ammunition, they bought more in town until there was not another cartridge available. Then, they simply withdrew.

Incredibly, not a single bullet struck Baca, presumably because he could lay a foot and a half below grade and return fire. He claimed to have shot and killed four of his attackers and wounded eight others. However, historical records say only one of the attackers died from a gunshot, and nobody could say from whose gun the shot had come.

In the light of the new day, the people who had stayed to watch the gunfight expected to find the corpse of Elfego Baca. Instead, they found the unperturbed deputy flipping breakfast tortillas on a wood stove leaking smoke from its many bullet holes.

Baca surrendered to Fransicquito Naranjo and was jailed on charges of murdering Young Parham and Bert Hearne. At his trial in August 1885, he was acquitted of killing Parham, whose death was listed as accidental, since Baca actually didn't shoot or kill him. When the court turned to the death of Hearne, witnesses testified to his confrontation with the deputy. They said Hearne had withdrawn his gun when he demanded Baca's surrender. That killing, too, was deemed self-defense, and the jury also acquitted him of Hearne's death, especially after Baca's lawyer entered the door of Armjio's *jacal* as evidence. The door had more than 400 bullet holes in it, amazing everyone the feisty Mexican deputy has survived the firefight.

Sadly, Baca didn't get to keep McCarty's *pistolas,* that would have added immeasurably to his swagger. He was also unable to stop the bullying and demeaning of his Mexican friends and neighbors.

Elfego Baca went on to live a storied life as a school superintendent, criminal lawyer, district attorney, political investigator for U.S. Senator Bronson Cutting, and even a bouncer of a Prohibition-era gambling house in Ciudad Juarez, across the Mexican-American border at El Paso. He was born at a time when the horse was the primary means of transportation. He died in 1945, at age 80, when he could have heard the roar of automobiles outside his house. And wild, lawless New Mexico finally had been — mostly — tamed.

Fabián Garcia — Horticulturalist
Number 9 changed more than just chili farming in Mesilla Valley

Every fall, the air in Mesilla Valley, in southern New Mexico, is redolent with the fragrance of roasting green chilis. It's an aroma with which many are familiar, but how many know the story behind the pepper.

Peter Koop, PhD, is director of the Department of Public History at New Mexico State University. He often lectures on the university's long and successful agricultural history, including one talk entitled "Replanting the Mesilla Valley: Fabián Garcia's Horticultural Legacy in a Global Context."

I graduated from NMSU in 1966. I had lived in Gracia Residence Hall and had done stories as a student journalist about the university's agricultural research. I knew Fabián Garcia's name, but I had never heard his story told so well.

Garcia came into his own as a world-renowned horticulturalist in the 1920s. It turns out he was the right man at the right time, and the story Koop told is not only about Garcia but about significant changes in Mesilla Valley agriculture.

For thousands of years, people who lived in the valley enjoyed its agricultural bounty. Paleo-Indian hunter-gatherers harvested wild plants and berries growing along the Rio Grandé. Cultivating plants changed people's lives. We often hear of descendants of the villagers living in pit-house communities and pueblos speaking reverently of the Three Sisters. Corn, beans, and squash were essential food stuffs for centuries. Wild cotton was also harvested, spun, and woven into fabric for clothing.

When the Spanish arrived, the Southwest changed forever, Koop says. "They introduced sheep, goats, cattle, and horses. They brought in grains like wheat, barley, and rye, grapes for making sacramental wine, and fruit trees, namely apples, peaches, apricots, and others. Being adaptive, native people integrated these into their own lives."

After the Spanish conquest of New Mexico, agriculture settled back into period of stasis. "For nearly four centuries, things changed very slowly," he says. The Anglo invasion began in the second quarter of the 19th century, culminating in 1846 with the Mexican-American War and United States' annexation of the Southwest. The nation was growing, and it needed to be fed. New Mexicans wanted a piece of the action.

Enter Fabián Garcia. Koop explains, "Garcia had been born in Chihuahua, Mexico, in 1871 and orphaned at a young age. His grandmother brought him to the U.S. and, after several homes in which she did domestic work, ended up in Mesilla as part of the household of Thomas Casad." Records show Garcia became a naturalized citizen of the U.S. in 1889.

Koop continues, "The Casads treated Fabián as their own. They provided a tutor and sent their servant's grandson to college."

In 1890, Garcia enrolled at New Mexico College of Agriculture and Mechanical Arts (today's NMSU) and was a member of the school's first graduating class in 1894. Koop says, "There are two interesting things seen in Garcia's class photo. There are four women," which was unusual enough. "And Garcia, who appears to be standing somewhat aside the group, apparently is the only Mexican-American. Without the Casad's support, he probably would not have been there at all."

Garcia attended Cornell University in Ithaca, NY, for a year and returned to New Mexico A&M to complete a Master of Science degree. "In 1904, he became a professor of horticulture and, in 1914, was named the first director of the state agricultural experiment station, a position he would hold until he retired in 1945," Koop says.

Remember, Koop adds, "This was taking place in a time when the nation was experiencing great changes"—changes that had begun in 1862. That year, President Lincoln marshaled four pieces of landmark legislation through Congress: the Morrill Land Grant College Act of which NMSU was a beneficiary, the Pacific Railway Act promoting construction of transcontinental railroads, the Homestead Act opening Western lands for farming, and the creation of the Department of Agriculture. "It was a pivotal time for a man like Garcia," Koop says.

Garcia had the vision to see how the introduction of specialty crops could benefit farmers, who were transitioning away from grains at that time. He began experimenting to find out what would grow best. By best, Koop explains, "Garcia was looking for plants that not only grew well and gave good yields but also were profitable."

The nation had a growing infrastructure. There were railroads to carry merchandise. There were canning technologies making it possible to preserve food for periods longer than in the past. All that was needed were the crops.

The signature crop for which Garcia is best know is the chili. Chilis are native to South America. They were part of the local people's diet as far back as 9,000 years ago. Archaeologists in Ecuador have found evidence chilis were domesticated at least 6,000 years ago. Over time, the peppers migrated with people throughout the Americas. For certain, the Spanish, whose native cuisine was already spicy, brought the peppers north into New Mexico—although, according to University of New Mexico's David E. Stuart in his book, *Anasazi America*, extensive trade patterns could have brought the pepper here much earlier.

Garcia experimented with three chilis, Koop explains, the Chili

Negro, Chili Colorado, and Chili Pasilla. "He created hybrids of the three peppers looking for one that produced a fleshy, smooth, tapering, and shoulderless pod. This would result in a chili that would peel easier after roasting and would be easy to can." Garcia's fame came in 1921, when a cultivar he modestly called *Number 9* became the chili he sought. "Number 9, the one we call the Sandia, was the pepper farmers needed, and it changed agriculture in the Valley."

Chili wasn't the only crop Garcia worked on. "He tested sugar beets, Acala cotton, and onions, notably the Grano that helped create the multi-million dollar sweet onion industry in Texas," Koop says. He also tested fruit, pecan, shade trees, and ornamentals.

Garcia died of Parkinson's disease in 1948, although his legacy continues in NMSU's Fabián Garcia Science Center, an agricultural research facility set on more than 40 acres of university land. The science center is at the location of Garcia's first labs, where he also once provided rooms for poor Mexican-American students working toward their degrees.

He bequeathed his entire estate to NMSU. Part of the money was used to build a dormitory in 1949, the same Garcia Hall I stayed in as a student in the 1960s. The bulk of his estate established annual scholarships for Mexican-American youth because, in Garcia's words, "I want to help poor boys, for I know their hardship."

Garcia's scholarship endowment was broadened in 1995, when the U.S. Department of Agriculture awarded NMSU $60,000 for a minority scholarship program. Funding for the Fabián Garcia Multicultural Scholars Program provides annual stipends for students preparing for careers in food science or agriculture.

Considered the father of the modern chili and Southwest food industry, Garcia was posthumously enshrined in the American Society for Horticultural Science Hall of Fame in 2005.

If you are a chili aficionado, you'll understand why a scorpion is part of Garcia's legacy. I'm not talking about an arachnid, but the Trinidad Moruga Scorpion, the world's hottest chili pepper until "Smokin'" Ed Currie, proprietor of the PuckerButt Pepper Company of South Carolina, developed the Carolina Reaper in 2013.

The heat of a chili pepper comes from capsaicin, a chemical with the unintelligible name (at least to anyone not a chemist) of 8-methyl-N-vanillyl-6-nonenamide or in symbolic terms, $C_{18}H_{27}NO_3$. Capsaicin binds to pain receptors in your mouth and throat. Once activated, the receptors send a message to your brain what's on your tongue is really, really hot. The brain responds by increasing your heart rate, making you sweat, and — this is the best part — releasing endorphins, a neurotransmitter resembling an opiate, giving you a feeling of well-being. Really. It's true!

Harvard psychologist Paul Rozin has likened eating chilis to riding one of these modern roller coasters; you know, the kind that go straight up and down for hundreds of feet while you're riding upside down. He says it's a "constrained risk." You can experience the extreme sensation and fear of the chili's heat, knowing what you are experiencing does not harm you in any way.

But, if the chili is overpowering and you're thinking of calling the EMT's, spoon sour cream on your tongue. The lactose in the cream binds with the capsaicin and puts out the fire.

Chilis are nutritionally high in B vitamins, potassium, and magnesium. They are also an excellent source of vitamin C, which increases our uptake of iron from other foods in a meal, such as beans and grains. Maybe that's why we always seem to put chilis in our *frijoles*.

The leaves of every species of *Capsicum*, the genus of plants that comprise peppers, are edible. They have no toxins in their leaves as do other plants in the nightshade family, of which *Capsicum* is part. The mildly bitter leaves, which are much less fiery than the pods, are common in Filipino, Korean, Thai, and Japanese cuisine.

But let's return to the *Scorpion* for a minute. The heat of a pepper is measured on a scale developed by American pharmacist Wilbur Scoville in 1912. The higher the number of Scoville Heat Units (SHUs), the hotter the pepper. Here are a few examples: Peperonicini – 900 SHU, Anaheim and Poblano peppers – 2,500 SHU, Scotch bonnet pepper – 350,000 SHU, and Red Savina Habanero chili – 580,000 SHU.

In 2007, the Bhut Jolokia pepper, developed at New Mexico State University, was listed in *Guinness World Records* as the world's hottest.

It's SHU number was 1.6 million. That's 400 times hotter then Tabasco sauce.

But the record stood for only four years. In 2011, NMSU produced the Trinidad Moruga Scorpion, which has some serious heat. It's Scoville number is 2 million. Now, the world's hottest pepper, the Carolina Reaper, sports a Scoville number of 2.2 million.

About the heat of the *Scorpion*, Paul Bosland, director of NMSU's Chili Pepper Institute, says, "You take a bite. It doesn't seem so bad. Then it builds and it builds and it builds." Your face turns red. Your eyes water. Your nose runs. And, for a moment, you're speechless—breathlessly speechless.

The reason for developing a chili that might set the house on fire is entirely in keeping with Garcia's original premise: find plants that not only grow well and give good yields but also are profitable.

Says Bosland, "You get more bang for the buck. A family could buy just two Trinidad Moruga Scorpions. That would be enough to flavor their meals for an entire week." Garcia would have appreciated this new development in chili peppers.

There are times when individuals see how the forces of community, industry, and government come together, and they change the course of history. People like Eli Whitney, Robert Fulton, and Orville and Wilbur Wright readily come to mind. Fabián Garcia is certainly to be numbered among them.

Sadie Orchard—Stage Driver and Madam
A Shady Lady with a heart to gold

She said she was from England, when she was actually born in Kansas. She said she learned her trade as a prostitute in London's Lime House District, although she would have been just eight years old at that time. She said she immigrated to the United States. Her British accent apparently convinced everyone or, more likely, no one cared enough to pursue the truth of her birthplace.

Sarah Jane Creech—she preferred to be called Sadie—said a lot of things during her life, many of which were simply untrue. Did she concoct stories to hide her past or protect her future? Did she want a life more adventurous than she had—which, as your read, will find hard to believe—and made up tales to convince others—and ultimately herself—they were true?

Whatever the case, Sadie Creech arrived in the mining town of Kingston in 1885, when she was in her twenties. Because prostitution, at that time, was more of an economic than a moral decision, she opened a brothel ironically on Virtue Avenue.

Despite her occupation, Sadie saw herself as a modest Victorian woman. She dressed in Victorian styles: dark stockings, ankle-length skirts with petticoats, and white shirtwaists. She wore her hair swept up in a bun, like most of the married women in town.

Within a year, she moved to Hillsboro to start another brothel. Hillsboro was county seat for Sierra County. A dozen miles to the east, it was less than ten years old then, established when prospectors Dave Stitzel, Daniel Dugan, and Joe Yankie discovered gold deposits along nearby Percha Creek.

Mining was booming in between 1882 and 1886. To the south, in Lake Valley, miners had uncovered the Bridal Chamber, said to be the richest silver deposit ever found. Its silver had the consistency of lead or putty in some places and could be cut into blocks by a hand saw. The mine yielded more than three million dollars in pure horn silver (nearly $75 million in today's currency). By 1886, the total silver production in the Lake Valley area would be 5.8 million ounces, with about half of that amount coming from the Bridal Chamber.

Sadie established her Hillsboro business as the Ocean Grove Hotel. She offered travelers lodging and served rich food and imported spirits. She also provided patrons with the inconspicuous company of young women. Literate and educated, Sadie was an astute businesswoman. She managed her two brothels, presented to the communities as hotels, as well as a boarding house, all of which seemed to prosper.

James W. Orchard, called Henry, operated a successful stagecoach line carrying passengers, mail, and cargo between Kingston, Hillsboro (which served as sort of a hub), Lake Valley, and Nutt, the railhead some 35 miles to the south. Sadie did what women since time immemorial have done. She flirted with Orchard until he had no choice but to propose to her. She had stolen his heart. They were married on July 17, 1895.

Henry formed a partnership with William Matthewson in 1894, a relationship in which Sadie took an active role. Now, in addition to her hotels and other businesses, she handled the Concord stagecoach and freight wagons carrying goods from Sears and Roebuck and Montgomery Ward, whose catalogs served as *dream-books* for families in the remote Black Range region. She made daily runs through creek beds and canyons where stages were vulnerable to raids by Apaches and robbers. One story relates horse thieves stopping Sadie, intent of relieving her of her team. Allegedly, she attacked them with her quirt and temper. The thieves left empty handed.

In an interview, Sadie said she and her husband ran the Orchard-Matthewson stage line for 14 years. "I drove four and six horses every day from Kingston to Lake Valley and sometimes as far as Nutt station," she said. She was, in fact, the first female stagecoach driver in New Mexico. Not only did she provide transportation for business people along the route, she escorted customers with discretion to her shady ladies.

The Orchards were married only five years, although Sadie frequently adjusted the truth to suit herself. They had three children, all of whom died young. Successfully bearing children wasn't their only problem. The marriage was like driving their stage over a rock-strewn trail. The *Sierra Advocate,* the local newspaper, reported this incident regarding an overturned carriage:

"Early Sunday morning, Mr. and Mrs. J.W. Orchard had difficulty over a carriage that had terminated, so it is alleged, in Mrs. Orchard taking a shot at Mr. Orchard with a revolver. Mr. Orchard had his wife arrested on the charge of assault with a deadly weapon with intent to kill and was taken before Justice Bickford Monday, but then the hearing was postponed until Saturday, Aug. 14th. On the other hand, Mrs. Orchard stoutly maintained the revolver was accidentally discharged while in the hands of Mr. Orchard. However, these counter allegations and the cause of their troubles will undoubtedly be diagnosed in the courts later on."

By 1900, the couple had separated. Sadie kept most of the property.

When people complained Kingston had 22 saloons but no church, a movement commenced to build one. In 1892, the cornerstone for the Union Church was laid, but there wasn't enough money to finish it. Sadie donated her diamond pendant and passed the hat among miners and gamblers, who frequented her establishments, to raise $1,500 to finish the stone church, in which she would never be welcomed.

On another occasion, a influenza epidemic roared through the community. Sadie and "her girls" nursed the sick. For babies who died, she paid for their burials and had coffins made, lined with silk from her petticoats. She used her own carriage to carry the caskets to the cemetery.

Her generosity extended to staking a miner, supporting a family fallen on hard times, and even buying books when the school needed them.

Now, you'd think the women of Hillsboro would not have looked down their nose at the generous madam from the Ocean Grove Hotel. Unfortunately, some did.

In 1907, Mrs. H. Kubale was arraigned on a charge of poisoning Sadie. A case of moral retribution or maybe just jealousy? It was alleged, Mrs. Kubale poisoned a glass of beer given to Sadie. Before she could drink, a disturbance outside distracted her. When she returned, she tasted her beer and found it too bitter to drink. Still the sip she had left her ill. Her doctor said there was morphine in the beer. Mrs. Kubale was arrested and later released for lack of evidence of a crime.

The question of Sadie Orchard's origin—and her honesty in relating the facts of her life—crops up time and again, especially in U.S. Census data. In 1900, the Census reported Sadie as a 38-year-old, married, though separated, English women, living in the United States for 30 years. So, how could she have learned her profession in London's Lime House district?

A decade later, she is listed as a divorced 43-year-old from England. Was her age reported incorrectly or was she just wanting to be five years younger?

The 1920 Census showed her at age 60 and reported her father was from Scotland and her mother from England. By 1930, she was listed as 68 years old, widowed, and proprietor of a hotel. This time she claimed both parents were from England.

Around 1930, Mae Creech Solday, Sadie's sister, and Martha M. Creech Norland, her niece, arrived in Hillsboro for a visit. Apparently, neither knew of Sadie's occupation as a madam or, more probably, just didn't care.

During the last few years of her life, Sadie was confined to her home, now reported as a "weather-beaten and deteriorated old hotel in Hillsboro." She died April 3, 1943. It doesn't appear the *truth* about her was very important when she died. Her obituary in the *Sierra County Advocate* made no mention of her shady past as a prostitute or the fact she had claimed to be from England. Her age was listed to be somewhere between 85 and 90 years.

Before her death, she was interviewed by Dr. A.C. White of Hot Springs (today's Truth or Consequence). Dr. White reported in funeral records, Sarah Creech has been born in Kansas on August 20, 1862, making her 81 years old at her death. The marker on her grave gives the dates of her life as 1865 to 1943, rendering her age at 78.

A letter a relative of Martha Creech Norland wrote to Ann Welborn, a former director of Truth of Consequences' Geronimo Springs Museum, reads, "My mother [sister to Sarah Creech] was there [Hillsboro] in the late 1920s or early 1930s. She told us about [Sadie] a long time ago but sounds like my Mom did not tell us everything."

Even in death, Sadie Orchard's story is frayed. Perhaps she had lived the lies she told so long she came to believe them as fact. She had to have known, in the end, people would know the truth about her, and maybe she didn't care. In its obituary, the *Advocate* referred to her as a colorful pioneer, but those who knew her and her story—knew her generosity and empathy for the people of Hillsboro—knew her as the shady lady with the heart of gold.

Black Jack Ketchum—Train Robber
The man who lost his head over his execution

Thomas Edward Ketchum, who became know as the outlaw "Black Jack," was born 1863 in San Saba, Texas, the youngest of eight children—six sons and two daughters. An older brother, Green Berry, Jr., established a successful cattle and horse ranch and became wealthy. Samuel, another brother, married, had two children, but then abandoned his family.

Thomas and Samuel worked in their younger years as cowboys on ranches from west Texas to northern and eastern New Mexico. Perhaps that's when the seed of getting rich fast from robbing rather than *pushin' horn* and eating dust for a living took root.

In 1892, the brothers learned the Atchison, Topeka and Santa Fe railroad stopped at a watering station just outside Nutt. It was the fruit on a low hanging branch they'd been looking for. Nutt is about halfway between Deming and Rincon, the latter being where a north-south line connected with the west bound through Deming onto southern California. Nutt was also the point of connection for a spur from Lake Valley, 20 miles north and site of the incredibly rich Bridal Chamber silver mine.

The Ketchums, along with Harvey "Kid Curry" Logan, his brother,

Lonnie Curry, and William Ellsworth "Elza" Lay, held up the train, getting away with a payroll of $20,000. During the robbery, the conductor sneaked away, made it to the station at Nutt, and telegraphed for help. Shortly thereafter, a posse from Lake Valley arrived, but the Ketchum gang by then was safely ensconced in their safe house. The $20,000 was never seen again...well, maybe it was and just not recognized.

While in New Mexico, the Ketchum gang liked to show off, attending dances and social functions and hanging out in saloons. Well-mannered, the young men rode good horses, dressed well, and flashed plenty of money they claimed they'd earned as cowboys. They frequented several establishments in Elizabethtown, about 40 miles west of Cimarron, where they also stayed at Lambert's Inn (today's St. James Hotel). No one knew until much later, these were the outlaws of Black Jack Ketchum's gang.

Meanwhile, Logan and Curry left the gang after a dispute concerning their share of the loot.

When not contemplating or engaged in robbery, the Ketchum brothers worked for the Bell Ranch, north of Tucumcari. But babysitting cows just wasn't what they wanted, so they stole supplies from the ranch and hightailed it.

On June 10, 1896, they rode into Liberty, a few miles north of Tucumcari, to buy supplies from the local store and post office operated by Morris and Levi Herzstein. That evening a thunderstorm struck the area, and the opportunity was just too much for the outlaws to resist. They returned to the store, where the Herzsteins had invited them to take shelter.

When Levi opened his store the next morning, he found both the store and post office had been burglarized. Herzstein and four others chased after the Ketchums who were riding hard for the Pecos River.

The posse caught the Ketchums by surprise in Plaza Largo arroyo, and a gun battle began. When the smoke cleared, Levi Herzstein and Hermenejildo Gallegos lay dead. Placido Gurulé was knocked from his horse by a bullet. With the wind knocked out of him, he lay semiconscious on the ground and watched Black Jack empty his rifle into the bodies of Herzstein and Gallegos. The fourth member of the posse, Anastacio

Borque had turned his horse and fled the arroyo. The Ketchums were never caught or tried for the murders.

Now marked as wanted outlaws, the Ketchums slipped into Wyoming where they joined Butch Cassidy in his Hole-in-the-Wall hideout in the Big Horn Mountains. Ketchum found Kid Curry and Lonnie Curry were also at the hideout. Kid Curry and Black Jack had such animosity for each other, Ketchum did his best to avoid him. That was perhaps a good thing, too, because Kid Curry killed nine lawmen over the next eight years. At a moment of anger, he probably would not have hesitated to plug Ketchum.

This story takes a turn here. The Ketchum gang decided to rob the Colorado and Southern Railroad near Twin Mountain between Folsom and Des Moines — New Mexico, not Iowa — at the point the Fort Union wagon road crossed the tracks. The location made for a clean getaway. They would wait until the train arrived at a hairpin curve just east of Folsom. The slow speed of the train at that point made it easy to board. Sometimes, they'd disconnect passenger cars and leave them stalled while the engine and mail and express car continued down the track, safe from intervention by any heroic riders. Other times, the passengers were fair game as well.

The Ketchum gang hit the train on September 3, 1897. Passenger Ike Mansker of Clayton told his fellow travelers they were involved in a hold-up and everyone should sit in the aisle in case a stray bullet was fired into the coach. Ketchum clubbed Charles Drew, the express messenger, and blew open the safe, took $20,000 in cash and $10,000 in silver. The robbers grabbed the large valise of Mrs. Thomas Owen, another passenger, and used one of her dresses to wrap up the loot. Then they fled to a cave near Folsom.

Ten months later, the Ketchum gang, including Elza Lay and Bill Carver from Cassidy's Wild Bunch, along with another robber named McGinnis, was camped at Daughtery Springs at the head of Dry Canyon, about four miles from the XYZ ranch. On July 11, 1899, they repeated their robbery of the train, making off with $50,000. This time, Black Jack wasn't in on the "fun." History doesn't make clear exactly where he was, but brother Sam robbed the train and headed into Cimarron Canyon, nearly 100 miles west of the robbery site.

George W. Titsworth, a law enforcement officer from Trinidad, Colorado, was given a letter torn into small pieces. He walked into a Folsom store owned by T.W. McSchooler and, with a glue pot, reassembled the letter. Then he had his men load their horses they'd brought from Trinidad on the train and rode to Cimarron.

There, a posse consisting of Sheriff Ed Farr of Huerfano County, Colorado, Special Agent W.H. Reno of the Colorado and Southern Railroad, and five deputies found the outlaws' trail and tracked them into Turkey Creek Canyon near Cimarron.

Posse and outlaws engaged in a gun battle. Sam Ketchum and his men were armed with high-powered rifles and smokeless powder. The posse only had shells packed with conventional black powder, which when fired revealed their positions and exposed the men. Sam Ketchum and two deputies were wounded seriously, but the gang escaped.

Ketchum's wounds slowed their getaway, and they made it only a short distance from the initial shootout before being cornered by the posse. In another gun battle. Sheriff Ed Farr was killed by a bullet that shot through the pine tree behind which he was hiding and struck him in the head. H.M. Love was struck by a soft-nose bullet that shattered his hip. He died a few days later.

McGinnis and Sam Ketchum both escaped but were found on a ranch a few days later and arrested by Special Agent Reno. McGinnis was tried, convicted, and sentenced to serve in the penitentiary at Santa Fe. Sam Ketchum developed gangrene from his wound and died two weeks later in the Santa Fe penitentiary. The Ketchum gang essentially was broken up.

Meanwhile, Black Jack, unaware of his brother's fate, decided to make a solo attempt to rob the train on August 16. He boarded the train from the blind side of the baggage car, planning to force the train to stop where he could disconnect the mail and express cars. Crawling into the engine cab, he forced the engineer and fireman to halt the train, but he'd miscalculated. Where the train stopped on the curve was a four-foot fill making it nearly impossible for the engineer to uncouple the train from the passenger cars.

Being robbed the third time was the last straw for Conductor Frank Harrington. He recognized Ketchum, grabbed his shotgun, and approached the baggage car. As he carefully slid the door open and poked his gun through, Black Jack saw Harrington and shot at him with his rifle. Ketchum's bullet went through the door, barely missing the conductor. At the same time, Harrington discharged his shotgun, hitting Ketchum in the right elbow and nearly severing his arm. Ketchum fell backwards off the train and down the bank of fill, momentarily escaping.

Harrington's gun muzzle was so close to the engineer, the blast from the gun burned the seat of his pants. The engineer grabbed his rear-end and yelled, "I'm shot. I'm shot."

Harrington ordered the engineer and fireman back to the engine and instructed them to get the train moving as fast as possible. Later he explained, "I wanted to hit the bandit in the heart, but in the dim light I misjudged. It had to be done quickly. I knew as soon as I opened the door, my appearance would be noticed by the robber who faced me, and I aimed the best I could."

Resuming the run, the train stopped at each station, reporting what had happened and sending word for law officers to look out for a badly wounded man near the scene of the hold up.

When captured Ketchum said, "I tried a dozen times to mount my horse but was too weak to do it." Weary and dizzy from the pain, he sat down to wait for the posse.

At sunrise the next morning, a freight train heading from Folsom passed by the robbery scene. They spied Ketchum sitting about 100 yards from the train. He had his hat on the end of his gun, waving it as a signal. The train was stopped, and the conductor and brakeman approached. Ketchum drew a gun on them. The conductor said, "We just came to help you but if this is the way you feel, we will go and leave you."

"No boys," Ketchum said, "I am all done. Take me in."

They carried him to the train, placed him in the caboose, and took him to Folsom, where Ben and Thomas Owen carried him to a local doctor for treatment of his wound. When he was able to travel he was transported to Trinidad. At the San Rafael Hospital, Ketchum had his arm amputated. He was returned to Santa Fe for safe keeping and later tried and convicted in Clayton.

The hanging was delayed several times because lawmen heard rumors the old gang was going to attempt to free Ketchum. They finally decided to execute him, and the hanging was scheduled on April 26, 1901, at 8:00 a.m. Ketchum told his jailers, after they had hanged him, bury him face down. "I want that conductor who shot me to kiss my ass for all eternity," he said.

Now, hangings in the Old West were a big attraction. Stores closed. Saloons remained open, doing a brisk business. People came from all over the area to see the big event. Local lawmen even sold tickets to view the hanging up close, as well as little dolls of Ketchum hanging on a stick.

However, Clayton had no experience in hanging a man, and there was a debate about how to do it properly. The night before the scheduled hanging, the rope was tested by attaching a 200-pound sandbag to the noose and dropping it through the trap. The bag was left hanging, stretching the rope until it was as rigid as a steel cable.

Finally, hours late, at 1:13 p.m. Black Jack Ketchum was led to the scaffold. The executioner placed over his head a hood that was pinned to his shirt. While they were adjusting the hood, Ketchum stated, "Hurry up, boys. Get this over with."

Sheriff Garcia's needed two blows from his hatchet to trip the trap door. Overweight and small-necked, when Ketchum dropped to the end of the rope, there wasn't any resiliency or bounce to soften his halt. Instead, the sudden stop yanked his head from his body. The black hood pinned to his shirt was the only thing that kept his head from rolling away.

A few minutes later Dr. Slack, the attending physician, pronounced him dead. The doctor then sewed Ketchum's head to his torso prior to the burial at the Clayton's Boot Hill. As requested, he was buried face down. Then, in the 1930's, his body was exhumed and removed to the new cemetery in Clayton, where it remains today.

Morris Herzstein, brother of Levi, killed by Ketchum, reportedly witnessed the hanging.

Black Jack Ketchum was the only person ever hanged in Union

County. He was also the only person in New Mexico who suffered capital punishment for the offense of "felonious assault upon a railway train." Later, the law was found to be unconstitutional. But the ruling was of no use to Thomas Ketchum.

According the annals of American Jurisprudence at the time, Thomas Ketchum was the only criminal decapitated during a judicial hanging in the U.S. The only other recorded example was in England in 1601.

Sallie Chisum — Cattle-woman-Entrepreneur
She was First Lady of Artesia

Walk through downtown Artesia, New Mexico, and you'll find seven, larger-than-life bronze sculptures. There are cowboys in various situations, oil drillers on a derrick floor, and two "good 'ole" boys talking over the fender of their pick-up. There's also a woman reading a book to a boy and girl, a sculpture done by artist Robert Summers.

That woman is Sallie Chisum, who came to be known as the First Lady of Artesia. The story she's reading was written by Pat Garrett in 1882 — *An Authentic Life of Billy the Kid*. (You can read about the last day of Pat Garrett's life elsewhere in this book.)

Sallie Lucy Chisum was born in Bolivar, Texas, in 1858. She had two brothers and a sister. When her mother and sister died, she was 19 years old. She, her father, and brothers went to live with her Uncle John in Lincoln County, New Mexico.

Uncle John turns out to be John Chisum, the man who built a ranching empire along the Pecos River. In the 1880s, Chisum ran 100,000 cattle over more than 50,000 acres. He called his outfit the Jinglebob Ranch. A jingle bob was a cut in a cow's ear, leaving a flap of skin dangling. It was nearly impossible for rustlers to alter as they could brands. John Chisum rarely worried about rustlers. Retribution was immediate and terminal. They pretty much left his herd alone.

Sallie Chisum arrived in this wild ranching scene and quickly established a presence on the Jinglebob. Uncle John was known for his hospitality at the Long House, his adobe headquarters. It was Sallie who supervised the ranch's two full-time cooks and dinner service for as many as 26 guests.

You may have heard of the Lincoln County War — a battle between the Lawrence Murphy-James Dolan gang and the John Tunstall-Alexander McSween gang, among whom was one William Bonney, better known as Billy the Kid. Murphy-Dolan ran a mercantile and had a monopoly in the county. John Tunstall opened a competitive store. When he was murdered, it set off the Lincoln County War.

Now, Billy the Kid sometimes cowboyed for Chisum; sometimes he used the Jinglebob as a sanctuary. He was known to rustle cattle and steal horses, so he occasionally needed a hideaway from the law.

When Sallie met Billy, they became instant friends. Stories tell she was loved by nearly every cowboy in Lincoln County, but Billy held a special place for her. They would often sit on the porch of the ranch house and talk well into the night. They also went on rides together, racing one another. Billy was an impulsive, adventurous young man, but I'd wager it was Sallie who instigated the races. Sallie said Billy was "The pink of politeness ... as courteous a little gentleman as I ever met." He was a year younger and may have been in love with Sallie, but she was smart enough to know nothing good could ever come from a union with the bad boy. And she was right.

The Lincoln County War erupted in 1878 and, among the violence, Sheriff William Brady was murdered. Billy the Kid was accused, although Brady's body had at least a dozen gunshot wounds from the six guns that had been aimed at him. That murder led to Billy's conviction in Mesilla and ultimately to his death by Pat Garrett at Fort Sumner in 1881. Garrett had been a sometime-friend of Billy and law enforcement that brought him to justice, thus his intimate knowledge of the legendary outlaw and the biography Robert Summers incorporated into his sculpture.

Meanwhile, in 1880, Sallie Chisum married William Robert, a

German immigrant. The couple moved to Chisum's South Spring ranch, south of the Jinglebob, where Robert worked as Chisum's bookkeeper. Sallie bore Robert three sons. The first, Reinhart, died at birth. Her other two sons, John and Fred, were raised on the ranch and, when old enough, their father sent them to Germany to be educated. When they returned to America, they had little to do with Sallie, apparently estranged from her.

When John Chisum died in 1884, his ranch was dissolved and the estate disposed of. Some of what was left went to Sallie. She moved to Chisum's Spring Line Camp along Eagle Draw, where she built an adobe house. It was swept away during a cloudburst that flooded the draw but, undaunted, she rebuilt it. For some years, she lived there with her father and two brothers, having been estranged from her husband. They officially divorced in 1895.

Sallie did not remain single for long but married Baldwin Gustav Stegman, a promoter and developer. Spring Line Camp was near a small community called Miller's Siding, established when the railroad came through Pecos Valley. It was named after Jeff Miller, a railroad engineer who operated a general store.

Stegman developed a hotel and other buildings attracting new settlers, who changed the town's name to Stegman in 1899. Sallie was appointed its first postmistress.

During her years with Stegman, Sallie augmented their income by renting rooms to travelers. A warmhearted woman, she often took in orphans and abandoned women who needed a place to live. She was known to be a fabulous storyteller, and the town's children were particularly fond of her, routinely visiting to hear her tales.

Her second marriage was no better than her first. She divorced Stegman and resumed calling herself Robert, though she and William were never reunited.

A resilient woman, Sallie had the *grit* early-day women needed to survive on their own. She successfully operated the hotel, made lucrative real estate investments, and kept her finger on the pulse of her ranch. She was said to be as good a cowboy as any man.

She also was responsible for the town's final and current name — Artesia. Sallie commissioned the first water well in the community. It turned out to be artesian, so abundant a source of water it drew settlers like bees to yucca blossoms. The name change to Artesia was made in 1903, and the town was officially incorporated two years later.

In 1908, Sallie built the first concrete-cast house in Artesia, which occupied the corner of Texas and 8th Streets—"Far enough away from Eagle Draw," she said, "to be safe from flooding."

Sallie lived in Artesia for nearly 30 years, until 1919 when she moved to Roswell. There, in 1932, she rode in the Old Times Parade. Unlike the cowboys she emulated, she rode side saddle as was her custom, wearing her old-fashioned riding habit. She rode straight and tall, commensurate of the pillar of the community she had become.

She died in Roswell at age 76 in 1934. The Old West in which Sallie had lived had vanished into history. It was time for her to join it.

On the occasion of what would have been Sallie's 146th birthday, Haley Klein, in her column for *The Artesia Daily Press*, wrote, "Her accomplishments as an entrepreneur, developer and woman led her to be known posthumously as First Lady of Artesia."

John Dunn—Lovable Rascal
Bridge across the Rio Grandé

"I've lived through the most dramatic period of history the West will ever see."

So said John Dunn in an interview he gave to J. Hogg in 1930. The interview is part of Max Evans' book, *Long John Dunn of Taos — From Texas Outlaw to New Mexico Hero*.

Visit Taos today, and you'll find the John Dunn Bridge, along county highway B6. You'll also encounter The John Dunn House Shops north of the plaza along a pedestrian walkway toward Bent Street. Shoppers nosing through a yarn shop and a book shop, in boutiques, or just enjoying a snack in the Bent Street Cafe may miss the historic significance of the building.

Born in Victoria, Texas, John Dunn worked his late teen years as a cowboy, driving herds over the Chisholm Trail. North of Kansas, *pushin' horn* to Canada, the land was still wild. He noted piles of buffalo bones some 20 feet deep, waiting to be ground for fertilizer, and river bottoms swarming with mule deer and antelope.

"A feller learned to use a rope," Dunn reminisces in Evans' book, "for more reasons than one. Sometimes it would save miles of hard riding after a steer...and it was handy to drag firewood to the cook, tie up a bronc, or even hang a man...out of necessity. The man, the horse, the rope, the gun became inseparable."

Back in Texas, Dunn ran afoul of the law. He was accused of killing his wife-beating brother-in-law in a fistfight. Convicted of manslaughter, he was sentenced to 40 years in the Texas penitentiary. He filed through his leg irons and escaped, evading recapture by hiding under a hay load en route to Taos.

Dunn landed in Elizabethtown, a gold mining camp between Eagle Nest and Red River. There he opened a saloon and gambling house, based on his experience at the roulette wheels and monte tables in Dodge City. From his time on the trail, he also dreamed of starting a transportation business, which he planned to finance from wealth earned from his gambling house.

Said Dunn, "If I could just find a place that was good and isolated and so damn rough it wouldn't pay to build railroads, I'd have just what I wanted."

What he found was Taos. The nearest railroad point was Tres Piedras on the Denver and Rio Grande line. Mail got to Taos only when someone happened that way. In 1890, Dunn purchased two bridges across the Rio Grandé in the bottom of the gorge, one at Taos Junction and the other at Manby Springs. Both were destroyed by flood, so around 1900 he built a new bridge west of Arroyo Hondo. That one burned and he replaced it in 1908.

Dunn got the contract to haul mail from Tres Piedras to Taos and started a lucrative stagecoach line, hauling passengers and freight. He owned the only stagecoach line in Taos for more than 30 years. When he bought the first automobile to Taos, he offered a taxi service.

Dunn charged toll to cross his bridge — a dollar for pedestrian, half a dollar for horses and cattle, a quarter for sheep. He averaged $250 a day in good years. That's about $6,500 in today's dollars, making him a wealthy man.

He added to his wealth by building a hotel at the bridge and scheduled stagecoach runs to arrive after dark, making certain passengers would lay over until morning. But he kept his customers happy by providing clean beds, milk from his own cow, and fresh trout his hired man caught for him. Among his patrons were artists, like Ernest Blumenshein and Mabel Dodge Luhan.

Regarding Dunn's relationships with people, Evans writes, Dunn said, "In handlin' the public as I've been doin' all these years, a fellow sees a great cross section view of the human animal. I've met so many worthless people I've often thought the world is bossed by an unjust God. A just God would have put fur on some of the people I've known. He'd have put skunk on some and beaver on others. Then they could be hunted in the winter for their pelts and be of some use to the rest of mankind."

Dunn sold his bridge to the state in 1912 and operated his stage line until the 1930s. He died in 1953. In his obituary which his old friend Doughbelly Price wrote for *El Crepusculo*, the journalist noted, "He had no education, but what he knowed was plenty and was learned from cattle, horses, natural observation and mother nature, the hardest, most tolerant and wisest teacher humanity ever had."

Dunn lived through three phases of the West: the gun fighting days, the cattle working days, and the present modern West. Evans writes, "Dunn said, 'Transportation made the West, not blazing guns as is so often preached — although I know guns played a big part. It was those sweat-stained horses and tireless mules, those worn saddles and creaking wagons and the men and women who were riding them across muddy rivers, rocky ridges and up those long dusty trails.'"

You can visit the old bridge today at the end of county highway B6, but you can't drive across it. The bridge was closed to cars in 2007 following a rockslide. Still, it's a great place for a summer picnic in the shade of the Rio Grandé gorge, and there are hot springs at Manby two miles to the south.

And while you scurry among the shops of John Dunn's residence between Taos Plaza and Bent Street, find a bench in the beautiful gardens and reflect a moment on John Dunn—bronc rider, stagecoach driver, saloon keeper, gambler, and lovable rascal...a New Mexico legend.

Sally Rooke—Folsom Heroine
For the price of a dime

Mrs. Sarah J. Rooke came to New Mexico from Iowa to visit her good friend, Dr. Virginia Morgan. Like many visitors to the Land of Enchantment, she fell in love with the West and, in 1906 at age 63, she packed up her things and moved to Folsom.

Not much was known about Sally Rooke. That's what her friends called her. She never spoke of her life back in Iowa. Except for the fact she was a member of the Order of the Eastern Star, an appendant body of the Masons, no one knew much about her, what had happened to her in Iowa, and why she felt compelled to move to New Mexico.

What was apparent was Sally suffered from scoliosis or curvature of the spine. There weren't many jobs she could do, but she found work as the switchboard operator for the town's phone system. A cheerful woman, she took great interest in her customers, inquiring about their children, their animals, their businesses.

Now, New Mexico has a monsoon season from late June through September. Even so, rain comes sporadically. Clouds build, towering over the land, their bottoms dark gray with the precipitation they carry. But too often they continue drifting east to drop their moisture on the Texas panhandle or farther still in central Oklahoma.

That was the situation in 1908. Drought had parched the New

Mexican grasslands. Blades of grass crunched underfoot like shards of broken glass. Just after a refreshing rain in the evening of August 27, the sun set on the happy, prosperous town of 800. But after sunset a strong southwest wind began to blow, and clouds began collecting over Johnson Mesa, eight miles west of Folsom. These low mountains provide drainage for what is known as the Dry Cimarron River. It's called dry because that's its condition most of the year. Near Folsom, the river is more of a trench, about ten to 15 feet across and ten or so feet deep.

Vivid and continuous lightning lit a background of solid gray clouds underneath a black and roiling mass of thunderheads. The storm so disturbed Sally's friend, Mrs. Edna Owen, she called to warn her of a possible flash-flood. But flash-flood wasn't in Sally's vocabulary.

Instead of heading for higher ground, Sally Rooke sat at her switchboard, giving warning to everyone she could contact. She didn't wait to hear what her friends and neighbors said, knowing most would question or argue with her. She couldn't wait. When people didn't answer, she worried, not knowing if they couldn't hear the phone ring or weren't at home.

One after the other she rang up to warn subscribers, but there were so many to call. So many who wanted to ask about the threatening flood, as if Sally had more information she could impart. So many who didn't answer. Sally hoped she'd be able to get through the board and ring those who hadn't answered the first time.

That August, hay had been cut and leftover stalks littered the fields. The cloudburst dumped an unusually large amount of water. It flowed across the ground, sweeping up stalks and other debris, which piled up against the small railroad bridge at Fisher Peak, creating an impromptu dam, much like beaver build. But the river was savage. It pounded the dam like a fist. Rocks beat against it, sounding like castanets. The dam could not restrain it. It burst. A wall of water, emitting the smell of drowned rodents, rotting hay, and other debris living and dead, surged into the dry stream bed. The trench-like riverbed quickly filled to capacity and then way beyond, growing to nearly a half-mile in width. It tumbled boulders the size of cook stoves. It tore at trees along the banks, dragging them into the torrent. Brown. Roiling. Angry. It surged into

Folsom. The river was rampaging. Berserk. It captured everything in its path. It left a wake of destruction unlike anything Folsom had ever seen.

Eyewitnesses on higher ground watched houses with families crying for help. Trees, shorn of branches and sanded of bark, pounded buildings like battering rams. Structural beams shattered, sounding like shot from hunting rifles. Relentlessly, the water swept them away. Some told of seeing lights flickering momentarily and hearing structures crash, crushed like egg crates. Some lights could be seen a distance of nearly a mile downstream before buildings were finally broken up and occupants drowned. An entire row of buildings was swept completely away. Others were jammed in a shapeless mass hundreds of yards from their foundations.

Sally continued calling people. Thanks to her, most people in harm's way made it to higher ground. More than 40 residents said they had received warning from her.

Then, she heard the rumble. At first, she thought it might be thunder. But this was different. Ominous. A rising bass building to crescendo. She knew the river was about to overtake her. She knew she had but a few more minutes. She knew she had to leave.

Like a moment from a Grimm's Fairy Tale, a bolt of lightning flashed over town, finding a wire strung between poles. It shattered the pole. Seared the line. Exploded the phone switchboard. It took from Sally Rooke her decision to flee. She was on the phone with Alcutt McNaughten and his mother, giving them warning. After the storm, McNaughten said he remembered hearing a loud crash and then Sally's voice ceased. The lightning claimed her life.

The river surged into the building housing the phone center and carried Sally's body away.

There were 17 people killed in the flood. Nine members of the Wheeler family died. Mr. and Mrs. Dan B. Wenger and their daughter, Daisy, were lost, plus Lucy Creighton, who kept books for Wenger's store. The Wenger house was seen with lights still burning floating down Grand Avenue. The screams of its four occupants could be heard above the roar of the waters. About two miles below town the flood waters created a whirlpool, which caught the Wenger house and spun it around until it hit the riverbank. After the flood, the largest piece of the house found was half of a door.

After the storm passed, after life in Folsom began to return to normal, the town's residents saw most of the buildings had been washed away. They found their livestock buried in the river bed, often only because a cow's legs protruded from the sand and gravel. They found the bodies of 16 people who'd drowned in the flood.

Several months later, Dan Harvey, whose property was a dozen miles downstream from Folsom, was clearing leaves and branches and other debris woven into dense mats where flood waters had overflowed the bank. In a sand bar, he saw a hand and exhumed Sally Rooke's body. Some have said the headset she wore to talk with her customers was still gripped in her hand. She was buried in the town's cemetery, the funeral paid for by Folsom's Masonic Lodge, since she was a member of the Eastern Star. But, since no one knew who Sally's relatives were, no one could be contacted. No one would claim the body. No one would mark her grave.

Folsom never recovered from the flood. Rather than rebuild, survivors simply moved away. Only about 80 people live there today.

Seventeen years after the Folsom flood, in 1925, *The Monitor*, the newsletter published by the Mountain States Telephone Company, related the story of Sally's heroic efforts to warn everyone about the flood. The article suggested her co-workers might like to contribute a dime apiece to erect a proper granite tombstone. Now, telephone operators, being the gregarious people they are, spread the idea by word-of-mouth, until every component of the former Bell Telephone System had heard.

In the early part of the 20th century, people paid a dime to make a call from a public phone. Operators across the country began collecting money, one dime at a time, for a memorial to honor their colleague. They collected 4,334 dimes, enough to pay for the marker.

In May 1926, a service was planned for the unveiling of the monument. People came from far and near. They were eager to share their story of how Sally's call had saved them or a loved one from the flood. Some shared how loved ones would have been spared had they only heeded Sally's warning.

Julie McDonald, author of *Unbreakable Dolls: True Stories of Amazing Pioneer Women*, wrote of Sally, "Indeed, if we remember she was no longer young, she was alone, it was night time, and she was contending with one of nature's most terrible forces, her strength of heart and purpose were superlative."

McDonald cites a contributor to the memorial from Boston, who wrote, "Love not duty: For it was not her sense of duty that held her there but love for her fellow-man. Such heroism and such devotion are the clear white lights which brighten the path of life and increase our faith. Would that we all might have as glorious a passing."

Pat Garrett — Notorious Sheriff
Leap Year wasn't a good time for him

For most people, February 29 is Sadie Hawkins Day, when girls get to ask boys out. For Pat Garrett, the notorious sheriff who gunned down Billy the Kid, the Leap Year day was not a good time for him. It was the day he died in 1908.

To fully appreciate this tale, you need the backstory of Garrett.

Patrick Floyd Jarvis Garrett was born in Alabama in 1850, one of seven children of John and Elizabeth Garrett. By the time Garrett was 19, the family had moved to Louisiana, and young Pat struck out on his own. He worked as a buffalo hunter, cowboy, and bartender. He met and befriended William Bonney, better known as Billy the Kid, often drinking and gambling with him.

In 1878, Garrett married Juanita Gutierrez, but she died within 12 months. A bit more than a year later, on January 14, 1880, he married Apolinaria, Juanita's sister. They would have nine children over the years.

Billy the Kid was implicated in the death of Sheriff William Brady during the Lincoln County War, implicated because Brady received a dozen gunshot wounds allegedly from at least six weapons. Still a bounty was placed on Bonney's head, and Garrett, who'd been appointed sheriff of Lincoln County, began the unrelenting pursuit of the outlaw.

Once captured, Bonney was tried and convicted of murder. The case was heard in Mesilla rather than Lincoln. He was returned to Lincoln to hang but escaped, killing two guards. Garrett was notified by Pete Maxwell Billy was hanging out in Fort Sumner at his friend, Silva's, house.

As Fort Sumner Mayor Justin Ingram tells the story: Billy got hungry. Silva told him Pete Maxwell has butchered a heifer. "Billy left his hat, jacket, boots, and gun at Silva's, but took a carving knife to go slice a piece of beef," Ingram said. "Now why would a man like Billy do that? He had a lot of friends among the Mexicans, and he felt safe."

Meanwhile, Garrett was conferring with Maxwell in his bedroom on July 14. He had also posted two deputies outside. They had never seen Billy, so they didn't identify the young man who came to the Maxwell place. Now Billy had a sweet spot in his heart for the ladies, one of whom was Celia Gutierrez, Garrett's sister-in-law who worked for Maxwell. "Perhaps he was looking for something other than beef," Ingram surmises. In any event, he thinks, Billy leaned through the door to Maxwell's bedroom. Sensing someone was there, he asked his now famous question—"¿Quien es?" "Who's there?" Garrett, of course, answered by shooting Billy twice in the heart.

While the *Santa Fe New Mexican*, perhaps the territory's most prominent newspaper, touted Garrett as a hero, most people saw him as the villain who killed their favorite son.

That may have been the turning point of Garrett's life. From that time on, everything the man attempted was doomed to failure. He served as a Texas Ranger but only for a few weeks. He lost his 1890 bid for Chaves County sheriff. He tried ranching in Uvalde, Texas, but was unsuccessful. He searched in vain for the murderers of Albert Fountain, whose killers have never been found after one and a quarter centuries. By 1901, he'd been appointed U.S. Customs Collector in El Paso. But he was drinking heavily and that, more than anything else, cost him that job.

Garrett had purchased a ranch in Bear Canyon in the shadow of

Mineral Hill about seven miles north of today's White Sands Missile Range headquarters. But the property had been heavily mortgaged. He owned back taxes and was unable to make mortgage payments. As a result, the county auctioned off all of Garrett's personal possessions to satisfy judgments against him. The auction netted only $650.

Destitute, Garrett left his family on the ranch and took a job with an El Paso real estate firm. Meanwhile, Dudley Poe, one of Garrett's sons, signed a five-year lease with Wayne Brazel, who was to run cattle on the land. Brazel had been in the employ of W.W. Cox, whose ranch headquarters was just about where the military base is now.

Only instead of cows, Brazel brought in a herd of goats. Cattlemen hated goats even more than sheep, and Garrett tried to break the lease. Brazel said he would agree to terminate the lease only if someone bought his goats.

Enter James Miller, a contract killer whose sister was married to Carl Adamson. In the popular language of the day, Miller would have been known as a gunslinger or a shootist. Miller sent Adamson to negotiate the transfer of the lease from Brazel to him, allegedly because Miller was holding rustled cattle in Mexico, and he needed somewhere else to hide them.

Adamson showed up at Garrett's ranch on February 28 to discuss the deal and spent the night. In the morning, Garrett kissed Apolinaria goodbye, climbed into a buckboard with Adamson, and headed west toward Las Cruces, where they intended to register the papers.

Along the way, they were overtaken by a lone rider on horseback. It turned out to be Brazel, who was to join them in town. So they rode together. In Organ, they rested their horses and then headed southwest toward Las Cruces. The road they traveled diverged from today's U.S. 70, entering town about where Hadley Avenue Sports Complex is on the geographic east side of town.

The three men argued about the goats. Adamson had agreed to purchase 1,200 animals. Just when they thought the problem resolved, Brazel said he had miscounted his herd, and there were actually 1,800. Adamson refused to buy that many but agreed to complete the journey to see if they could reach some kind of agreement.

About halfway between Organ and Las Cruces, where the road crossed the Alameda arroyo, Adamson stopped for a call of nature. At this point, Garrett's and Brazel's discussion turned heated. Garrett said, "If I can't get you off one way, I will sure try another!" implying he'd kill him.

What happened next is pure speculation. Brazel claimed Garrett aimed his shotgun at him. He pulled his six gun and shot him. The shotgun was on the floor, and Garrett would have had to bend over to get it. That first bullet entered the back of Garrett's head on the left and exited his right eye. Hearing the shot, Adamson turned and watched Brazel shoot again, this time firing a bullet into Garrett's chest as he fell from the buckboard.

Adamson told Brazel he should continue into town and surrender to the sheriff. He did, and Deputy Sheriff Felipe Lucero arrested him and put him in jail.

A posse, led by Major Eugene Van Patten, proprietor of Dripping Springs Resort, searched the killing site and brought Garrett back to town. It is said the cart in which he was carried was so short, Garrett's feet hung out and the heels of his boots were worn away from dragging on the ground. His shotgun had not been fired. Investigator Captain Fred Fornoff of the New Mexico Mounted Police found unexplained hoof prints, horse dung, and an empty Winchester rifle shell casing at the site, indicating another shooter.

Brazel was charged with first-degree murder. His trial began in April. The accused was defended by Albert B. Fall, who had represented Oliver Lee and Jim Gilliland in the murder trial of his nemesis, Albert Fountain. Lee and Gilliland had been acquitted and, now after one day, Brazel was also acquitted.

James Miller could not testify. He had been killed in a duel. Carl Adamson was unavailable, having been convicted of smuggling and incarcerated in the Arizona Territorial Prison. Brazel convinced the jury beyond reasonable doubt he had acted in self-defense. Fornoff's additional evidence was considered irrelevant.

After the trial, Brazel left the area. He is supposed to have married and moved away. No one ever heard from him again.

Stories like this always have an aside or two. This one is no different.

When Wayne Brazel shot Pat Garrett, his wife, Apolinaria, is said to have screamed, "They've killed him," and fainted. She was still on the east side of the Organ Mountains.

The controversy over Garrett's death continued long after he was buried in the family lot in Las Cruces's Masonic cemetery. Was this a single act by an irate Brazel, who felt himself threatened, or were others involved? Some have claimed Albert Fall, W.W. Cox, Lee and Gilliland, and even Adamson or Miller fired the killing shot.

The iconic truth is "Dead men tell no tales." Garrett is unable to unravel the conspiracies that swirl around him. In the Masonic cemetery, a short walk from the Garrett family lot, is a stone bearing the cenotaph for Albert Fountain and his son, Henry, whose disappearance and presumed murder Garrett had investigated. No one has ever found their bodies.

At least, we know where Pat Garrett is buried.

George McJunkin — Curious Cowboy
His discovery changed New World archaeology forever

Following the Civil War, tens of thousands of men were discharged from the armies. In the South, it was unthinkable for a black man to get equal treatment for work as a white man. In the North, white men didn't relish the idea of the competition. To alleviate the tension, the army formed cavalry and infantry units for African-Americans and moved them to the West, where they became known as Buffalo Soldiers, thus, reducing the pressure on the overburdened Eastern job market.

However, George McJunkin was already in the West. In 1851, he had been born a slave in Midway, Texas, about 100 miles northwest of Houston. His father had been a blacksmith, and McJunkin learned the trade. He also had grown up around horses, learning to ride and rope.

When the war ended and he was freed, at age 14, McJunkin joined a cattle drive bound for Dodge City, Kansas. He left Texas for good, never looking back. Brenda Wilkinson, a field archaeologist with the Bureau of Land Management, writes, "Along the way, he stopped to help a man dig a well. He earned a handful of quarters, the first money he had ever been paid for his work. He used it to buy the first footwear he had ever worn—a used pair of cowboy boots." He also managed to obtain a wide-brimmed hat, jeans, and a used saddle.

McJunkin assisted trail cooks, learned to tell time by following night stars, and survived stampedes. He learned to read, often breaking horses for reading lessons. He also learned Spanish, played a mean fiddle and, we're told, had an unquenchable curiosity, especially for the natural world around him.

In the interim years, McJunkin worked as a freighter and as a cowboy on ranches in Colorado and New Mexico, reportedly becoming an expert bronc buster and an even better roper. Some said he was the best roper in America. That earned him a job as foreman at the Crowfoot ranch near Folsom, New Mexico.

He settled into life in New Mexico's Dry Cimarron Valley in the 1880s. Although African-Americans had migrated from the east or left the army in search of a better life, New Mexico was not colorblind. Many of the men McJunkin supervised, called him Nigger George, a sobriquet most likely attached to him because the rancher for whom he worked had been a slave owner and never allowed McJunkin to eat with his family. Despite the prejudice and discrimination, McJunkin enjoyed a level of success unimaginable in the South.

Because he was often ostracized for his color—and maybe because he simply preferred his own company—McJunkin built a cabin in which to live. It also became the repository for the things of nature he found while working.

Being a cowboy meant long hours of solitude in the saddle, riding fence. Large ranches, like the Crowfoot, had miles and miles of barbed wire fencing. Animals could push against it and break a post. Storms could uproot trees that crumbled wire or undermine posts with heavy rainfall. Riding fence was something cowboys did a lot of, and they often rode alone. It didn't take more than one man to mend a broken wire or set a post.

To alleviate the boredom, McJunkin indulged his interest as an amateur naturalist and archaeologist. Riding the grasslands of northeast New Mexico, he was likely to find pottery shards, arrowheads, and other artifacts left behind by people who had previously occupied the land.

On August 27, 1908, a cloudburst occurred west of Folsom. The banks of the Dry Cimarron River, called dry because that was its usual state, filled to overflowing with a violent flood that claimed 17 lives. (See the story in this book about Sally Rooke and the flood.) When the water receded, McJunkin left to assess damage to the ranch.

He rode into Wild Horse Arroyo, a side drainage of the Dry Cimarron. It had been severely incised by the raging rainstorm. In the arroyo's embankment, he found some bones. Now, that wouldn't have been uncommon in cattle country. Cows often died, were consumed by wolves, coyotes, and other scavengers, leaving their bones to be buried by windblown sand or storm sediments.

However, these bones appeared to be from a bison, also not uncommon considering the millions that once roamed Western grasslands. But they were bigger than any bones McJunkin had ever seen. As he examined the site, he noted a stone tool with the bones. He had discovered the remains of a giant bison gone extinct at the end of the last Ice Age. The fact the stone tool was with the bones proved humans, who had killed the animal, had existed on the plains far earlier than anyone had thought.

Recognizing the significance of the find, he left the site undisturbed — instead, writing an expert in Las Vegas, New Mexico, who had studied mammoth and other ancient animals.

Now, perhaps the so-called expert didn't believe McJunkin. He was after all just a cowboy. Perhaps the expert had no financial resources to study the site or needed time to organize an excavation.

When nothing happened, McJunkin and Bill Gordon, a cowboy friend, sent some of the bones to people in Raton, who expressed interest in evidence of extinct animals.

McJunkin died in 1922, and no one had shown much interest in his find — until seven months after his death. That was when Carl Schwacheim, one of the people in Raton whom he had notified about the site, and Fred Howarth, a Raton banker, along with a Roman Catholic priest and a taxidermist finally visited Wild Horse Arroyo. They were amazed at the bones eroding from the embankment and began to survey the area and make notes.

Their interest sparked the interest of J.D. Figgins, an archaeologist at the Colorado Museum of History—now the Denver Museum of Nature and Science. Figgins hadn't seen bones like these before and knew McJunkin's find was important.

In 1926, he and Harold Cook, another archaeologist from the Colorado museum, began excavation of what they now called the Folsom site. Their work exposed bones from at least 30 extinct bison, named *Bison antiquus*. It had never before been described in scientific literature.

A year later, they made an even more important discovery. They found a stone spear point—they now called the Folsom point—stuck between the ribs of the extinct bison. McJunkin had come upon a kill site of Stone Age hunters, indicating people were living in the Southwest more than 11,000 years ago, a much longer timespan than scientists had previously thought—and that timeline has been pushed even farther back with more recent discoveries.

The Folsom point is a distinctive type of tool, requiring great technical ability to effect. It has a symmetrical, leaf-like shape with a concave base, making it possible to firmly bind to a spear or dart. Worked on both sides, it also has wide, shallow grooves, known as fluting, running nearly its entire length, and fine, extremely sharp edges.

The Folsom site was the first generally recognized as evidence of the great antiquity of human habitation in North America, and it set off a huge wave of interest in archaeology in the Southwest and the Pleistocene period in general. George McJunkin had changed New World archaeology forever.

But his contribution wasn't widely recognized until almost 50 years after his death, when George Agogino of Eastern New Mexico University heard stories about him from people living in the Folsom area. Agogino tracked down and recorded stories from those who knew the ex-slave cowboy turned amateur archaeologist.

George McJunkin never married and had no children. He died in his bed at the Folsom Hotel at age 71 and was buried in Folsom's cemetery.

That might be the end of this story, except for what Brenda Wilkinson writes — almost as an epitaph.

"His hunger for knowledge and his persistence eventually earned him a special place in history."

New Mexico, 47th State Period

1912-Present

Clyde Norman—Merchant
New Mexican Pie-oneer

In 1922, Clyde Norman, a World War One veteran from Texas, was looking to make his fortune. It just may be he was also looking for a life that didn't include the pressure and chaos of civilization that had brought America into the European war. In short, Norman sought the freedom to leave where he was to try and make it in another place. It's a story that would repeat itself thousands of times in the next two decades.

Norman was traveling along the dirt road that would become U.S. 60, running coast-to-coast from Virginia Beach to Los Angeles, when his car broke down, stranding him astride the Continental Divide. He must have thought it fortuitous. He was just south of the Datil Mountains, so he made plans to stay.

He filed a mining claim on 40 acres of juniper and piñon-dotted land and went to work as a prospector and miner. But gold and silver ore was not the wealth he would find, especially since he never extracted enough to make it worthwhile.

Meanwhile, Norman needed to earn a living, so he turned his place into a general store. Besides the sundries he offered, he sold kerosene for people's lamps and gasoline. People frequently needed a fill-up along the rural stretch of the highway. He was, after all, half way between Socorro, New Mexico, and Springerville, Arizona, nearly 8,000 feet above sea level on the Divide but still in the middle of nowhere.

Once again, success eluded him. His general store earned him barely enough to get from month to month. But Norman also loved to bake pies. Actually, he loved to eat pies and, to do that, he had to first bake them.

Besides the growing auto traffic through the area, there was a "hoof" highway, the Magdalena Livestock Driveway running from Springerville to the railhead in Magdalena, 30 miles west of Socorro.

In its peak year of 1919, 150,000 sheep and 21,000 cattle were driven along the trail. During the drives, cowboys moved cattle about ten miles a day and herders moved sheep about five miles, allowing them to graze as they went. Chuckwagons and relays of horses followed behind.

Norman wasn't the only one who loved pies. Cowboys and herders, tired of beans, biscuits, and spotted pup, the ubiquitous chuckwagon rice pudding with raisins, traveled an hour or so to Norman's place. Soon, they'd tell each other, "You get over to Pie Town and get some of Clyde's pies. Best you'll ever eat."

Reputations were built on less, and Clyde Norman's general store morphed into a pie emporium; a village began to spring up around it—a place called Pie Town. Despite objections from the government, who thought the name too unconventional, it stuck.

When you think about it, Norman *was* isolated. He was far from sources of supply. Albuquerque, for example, is 160 miles north. His business grew by word of mouth. He had no advertising budget and, even if he had, there were few places where he could have advertised. Just surviving until he could turn a profit must have taken a lot of grit. But Clyde Norman, a man with a mission to make pies in the middle of nowhere, succeeded because it never occurred to him he couldn't.

In 1924, Harmon Craig purchased a half-interest in Pie Town. A few years later he bought out Norman's remaining interest. The people of Pie Town petitioned for a post office in 1927. When the Postmaster General suggested they find a more dignified name, they refused.

By the 1930s, the Great Depression was at its darkest moment. People fled the Dust Bowl of Texas and Oklahoma. Some settled on homesteads around Pie Town, looking for that elusive freedom to leave where they were and make it in another place. Craig now controlled the little town, owing the general store, a cafe, gas station and garage, and a pinto bean warehouse. He often helped struggling homesteaders, selling land below market value and making loans that required no collateral and charged no interest. In addition, his bean warehouse provided dryland farmers with a way to market their crops.

Clyde Norman was gone by then, but he had left his indelible mark astride the Continental Divide. As travelers race along Interstate 40 to the north, Pie Town remains far off the beaten track, but adventurous souls, willing to wander a less traveled road, can still find a slice of their favorite pie in the cafes along the highway.

James Larkin White — Cavern Dweller
The man who swapped cows for caves

" I want to be a cowboy."

That's how ten-year-old James White answered his father in 1892 when challenged about why he was playing so much hooky from school. Most fathers would have smiled and told their sons they could be what they wanted to be when they grew up. Now was the time for school.

Instead, Jim White's father took him from their Mason County, Texas, home nearly 400 miles to the ranch of John and Dan Lucas, just west of Eddy — today's Carlsbad. There he left him to learn to be a cowboy. Left him but did not abandon him. White's father bought a small parcel of land three years later and raised horses nearby the Lucas' ranch. Young Jim occasionally came home but mostly stayed and worked the ranch. He was living his dream.

About the time he was 16, White was riding fence, mending breaks, and looking for strays in arroyos west of town. What he saw would have stopped anyone dead in their tracks. It did him, too. A column of smoke appeared to be rising from a ridge line to the west. He knew that could mean only one thing — wildfire — and he needed to determine how big it was and in which direction it was burning? The ranch and livestock depended on it.

As he got closer, he got confused. He could see smoke, but he couldn't smell it. And he could neither hear the crackling of burning bush nor feel the heat of fire. He didn't like what he saw. Neither did his horse. He tied his pony to a nearby tree and began working through the cacti and sage to the top of a ridge in search of the blaze. The last thing cowboys want to do is abandon their horses and go on foot. White had no alternative and climbed until he came upon a large opening in the ground.

What he had seen wasn't smoke from wildfire. It was a plume of thousands and thousands of Brazilian free-tailed bats rising from the opening. He thought, any hole in the ground that could house a gigantic flight of bats had to be huge, and he found himself gazing into the biggest and blackest hole he'd ever seen, out of which the bats seemed to boil.

Park Ranger Lacey Thomas wrote on the Carlsbad Caverns National Park blog, "Because he knew the other cowboys would mock him, Jim didn't immediately describe what he'd seen to anyone. He thought it over for several days. The deep hole in the ground and its secrets continued to gnaw at him."

Now, any ten-year-old who'd give up school to follow his dream of cowboying has to be an adventurous soul. White was no exception, and Ranger Thomas adds, "He just had to find out what was down in the dark recesses."

White returned to the cave a few days later. He had some rope, fence wire, and a hatchet. He cut some nearby trees, probably mesquite, and made a ladder. He also lit his hand-made kerosene lantern. Then, he descended 60 feet to the cavern floor, one hand on the ladder and one on his lantern, which barely penetrated the cloying darkness.

If you've visited Carlsbad Caverns, you know—during the tour—the Park Ranger sits you down on a low wall and douses the lights. For the first time in your life, you know the meaning of absolute darkness. There's not a single photon of light to excite the cells of your retina. You put your hand in front of your face, but you can't distinguish fingers from background, even when your palm touches your nose. It's the perfect setting for instantaneous claustrophobia. If you weren't already sitting, you'd probably keel over.

Now, imagine Jim White crawling all alone through that darkness. At the point where he entered the cavern, he discovered two tunnels. He examined one leading to the bat cave. Then he explored the other, following a path cut by water. His weak lantern illuminated strangely beautiful formations: stalagmites, stalactites, rim-stone dams, soda straws, and chandeliers. White found them fascinating, if somewhat frightening.

He was the very first person of European descent ever to see them. Zuni and Mescalero Apache had known of the cave for generations, although there is no evidence they ever explored them. There are mescal cooking pits and petroglyphs in the area around the caverns. White said, "I knew instinctively there was no other scene in the world which could justly compare with my surroundings."

A week later, he returned to the cavern with a 15-year-old Mexican boy he called Pothead. That may have been because of the shape of the kid's skull and not what he smoked. For three days, the two young men explored the caverns, carrying food, water, fuel, and handmade torches. They also smartly unwound a ball of string as they wandered underground, the better to find their way out.

At first, they were uncomfortable in the dark. The names White assigned to the formations reflect their anxiety. He named the first drip pool *Devil's Spring*. That was soon followed by the *Devil's Armchair, Devil's Den*, and finally the *Witch's Finger*. As White explored and became comfortable being underground, he named other formations—now-familiar names like *The Big Room, Queen's Chamber, King's Palace,* and *Green Lake Room*.

Among the places White named was *Bottomless Pit*. He had been crawling along a ledge next to a wide and seemingly deep pit. He threw a stone over the edge and listened for it to hit bottom. No sound ever came back to him. He assumed it had no bottom or was so deep sound dissipated before reaching him. Many years later, other explorers determined the *Bottomless Pit* indeed did have a bottom. It was 140 feet down, and stones cast over the side fell onto a bed of soft dirt, absorbing the sound.

Once word got out, two things happened. One involved deep deposits of bat guano; the other was people wanted to see the formations White described on his excursions into the heart of the Guadalupe Mountains.

High in nitrogen, guano is a perfect fertilizer and was sought by California farmers for their fruit orchards. A guano mining company was formed, although its name is lost to history. Hopefully, White had an interest in the enterprise. He would have made considerably more money mining than cowboying.

For those more interested in sight-seeing than digging fertilizer, White found an unusual accommodation. The guano diggers used a large iron bucket, powered by a gasoline winch, to raise bags out of the cave. White used the bucket to lower and raise hundreds to tourists into the cave, where—for a fee—they could see the spectacular formations. He continued using the guano bucket until 1925, when a wooden staircase was built to allow tourists into the cavern. The staircase can be seen on today's tours, but it is no longer sturdy enough to be used.

Jim White eventually gave up his dream of being a cowboy for more heady enterprises. He continued exploring the caverns for many years and is credited with devoting his life to promoting them. Carlsbad Caverns was named a national monument by President Calvin Coolidge in 1923. Seven years later, Congress passed a bill upgrading the caverns to a national park. The bill was signed into law by President Herbert Hoover.

Ranger Thomas concludes her blog, "Carlsbad Caverns National Park owes its existence to the bats, who call this place home, and a young cowboy who just had to know more about the dark hole that teased his imagination."

Arthur Hannett — Governor
He got the last laugh

It's called the Mother Road, a moniker applied to the historic U.S. highway labelled as U.S. Route 66. The highway stretches from Chicago to Los Angeles and traverses the entire 375-mile width of New Mexico.

We like to think of Route 66 shooting straight across the state because that's how Interstate 40 is today, and we know it followed the Mother Road. But, in its early years, the road itself was as convoluted as its history.

In the early 1920s, the last decade of America's Golden Age, the nation was developing a network of national highways. One of its most ardent promoters was Cyrus Avery of Tulsa, who knew a national highway would bring greater prosperity to Oklahoma. U.S. 60 had been laid out from Virginia Beach to Springfield, Missouri. It was slated to continue across Kansas, Colorado, and Utah to California.

Avery had a different idea. He wanted the highway to run from Springfield through Tulsa, Oklahoma City, and Amarillo. It would enter New Mexico at Glenrio, travel to Santa Rosa, and then southwest to Vaughn, Encino, Mountainaire, Socorro, and Quemado before entering Arizona. He promoted the route as avoiding crossing the high Rockies in Colorado. Moreover, he thought the road should extend north to Chicago, believing that would give Oklahoma ranchers better access to Chicago stockyards.

In 1926, the U.S. commissioned Route 60 the way Avery wanted — all except the part from Chicago to Springfield. He had been opposed by highway commission members of southern states who wanted an Atlantic to Pacific highway.

That's where our story of Arthur Hannett's Joke begins.

Arthur T. Hannett had been a controversial trial lawyer, mayor of Gallup, and member of the state highway commission before being elected governor, serving from January 1925 to January 1927.

According to Eric Scott Jeffries, who wrote *The Historic Committee Presents - Hannett's Joke: Route 66* for the *Bar Journal* in 2000, New Mexico was a rapidly changing world. Its politics were as rough and tumble as its roads. When Republican Bronson Cutting was U.S. Senator, he accused the Hannett administration of corruption.

Jeffries wrote,"Cutting charged Gov. Hannett with 'stealing the election from Manuel Otero two years ago; with having double-crossed the candidate for treasurer; with being unfair to Spanish Americans in the selection of Ed Scope as a successor to Land Commissioner Justina Baca; and with using the office for the benefit of a little ring calling itself the Democratic Party.'"

Hannett lost the 1926 election to Republican Richard Dillon, a sheep rancher from Encino. The now-lame-duck governor apparently decided he had time to seek revenge for the political slight he perceived to have suffered.

Shortly after the November election, Hannett called E.B. Bail, state highway engineer, to his office. He placed a map before the engineer and drew a straight line from Santa Rosa, through Moriarty, to Albuquerque. Bail was familiar with this suggested route. A Mr. Crossley of Moriarty had once driven Bail over the cross-country route.

This is where Hannett said he wanted to new U.S. highway built. It by-passed Encino and put Governor-elect Dillon's sheep ranching business in jeopardy. The highway engineers were enthusiastic about the challenge. They knew they would lose their jobs on the first of January and thought the project a huge joke.

Hannett had Bail assemble two crews: one Bail led east from Moriarty; the other led by Sam Fulton west from Santa Rosa. In 31 days, the crews surveyed, cut, scraped, and graded 69 miles of highway. They worked through bitter December weather. They worked with a makeshift collection of tractors, graders, and dilapidated World War I caterpillars.

Bail's Moriarty crew encountered nearly 30 miles of piñon forest. They chained trees to tractors and yanked them out of the ground. They cut fences without obtaining condemnation notices. Apparently, landowners thought the road would benefit them. There was not a single law suit filed.

On January 1, 1927, Governor Dillion sent his highway engineer to Palma, about halfway between Moriarty and Santa Rosa, to stop construction. But a heavy snow storm prevented him from reaching the road crews before January third. By then, the two crews had met; the road was finished.

That should be the end of our story. But it's not.

The southerners opposing Cyrus Avery won and got their sea-to-shining-sea highway. It took until 1932 to complete U.S. 60 from Springfield through Amarillo to Clovis, Vaughn, Encino and the rest of the route we can drive today.

The proposed Chicago to Los Angeles highway was numbered Route 66. But, instead of following Hannett's Joke from Santa Rosa to Albuquerque, it met the interests of Santa Fe politicians, business people, and the tourist industry. Route 66 left Santa Rosa in a northwest direction to Romeroville, just south of Las Vegas. It turned south through Glorieta Pass to Santa Fe, switchbacked down La Bajada Hill to Albuquerque, and farther south to Los Lunas. There it turned northwest again, avoiding the worst of the steep, sandy escarpment of Albuquerque's west mesa, to Correo before heading to Arizona.

Route 66 wasn't completely paved until 1937, New Mexico being a recipient of Works Progress Administration funding to ameliorate the impact of the Great Depression. The National Recovery Act of 1933 allotted nearly six million dollars for road work in New Mexico, including new bridges, paving, grade crossing elimination, and roadway straightening.

This last task—roadway straightening—had its highlight in 1937. That's when the state highway engineers decided to realign Route 66 and cut more than a hundred miles off the route. The giant "S" that swept nearly to Las Vegas and then to Los Lunas was eliminated. The road was realigned directly from Santa Rosa to Moriarty to Albuquerque—following Gov. Hannett's rush job at the end of his administration.

I guess you could say Arthur T. Hannett finally did have the last laugh.

Clyde Tombaugh—Astronomer
The man who discovered Planet X

The images of the distant sky continued to blink as the comparator flipped from one to the other. Nothing moved. Stars are so far away, their velocity measured over a period of six months is minuscule. The astronomer had been looking at the glass photo plates night after night. He was searching for Planet X.

Not long after Uranus was identified in 1781 by English astronomer Sir William Herschel, it was discovered to have unusual movements that could be attributed only to another planet. Sixty-five years later, Neptune was found by German astronomer Johann Gottfried Galle—based on observations of Frenchman Urban Le Verrier and Englishman John Couch Adams — but there were still orbital discrepancies unaccounted for.

In 1905, Percival Lowell, who had built the Lowell Observatory in Flagstaff, Arizona, began a search for the elusive Planet X. The principle method of identifying distant planets was the use of the blink comparator. Two photographs of the same segment of sky taken months apart were inserted into the machine. It projected the two images, blinking from one to the other. Stars, as noted, didn't move — at least not far enough to matter. A planet, however, circling the sun would have moved appreciably, and its tiny pinpoint of light would flicker.

The plates the astronomer was studying registered the light of 150,000 stars — sometimes his plates recorded nearly a million. Week after week, month after month, he searched the sky.

Rubbing his eyes, fatigued from staring at the comparator, he suddenly stopped. He blinked the machine again, and again, and again. One of the dots of light danced before his eyes. Was it real? Or were his eyes so tired, he couldn't tell? He took a couple minutes to rest. He stood and stretched. Then he huddled over the comparator and looked again.

On February 18, 1930, Clyde William Tombaugh had found Planet X. On his discovery, he said, "I thought I'd better check this third plate, which is another date, to see if there's an image there in the right place that would be consistent with the images on the other plates. That was the final proof." Sadly, Percival Lowell had died 14 years earlier, in 1916. He never got to see the planet in which he had invested so much of his time, energy, and money.

With the discovery came the right to name the planet. The Lowell staff made a worldwide call for suggestions. They selected the name offered by Venetia Burney, an 11-year-old English schoolgirl. She recommended Pluto after the Roman god of the underworld. Everyone seemed to be in agreement, except perhaps Tombaugh, who had wanted to call it Lowell's planet. He had to be satisfied the first two letters of Pluto were P and L. The name was officially adopted by the International Astronomical Union (IAU) on May 1, 1930, a name that endured for more than 70 years before other similar celestial objects were found in the Kuiper Belt, where Pluto resides, and it was demoted to a *dwarf* planet.

Tombaugh's widow, Patricia, said while her husband may have been disappointed—he had resisted other attempts to remove Pluto's planetary status over his lifetime—he would have accepted the decision. After all, he was a scientist. Hal Levinson, a planetary scientist at the Southwest Research Institute in Boulder, Colorado, said, "Clyde Tombaugh discovered the Kuiper Belt. That's a lot more interesting than the ninth planet."

But we're gotten ahead of the story and that's never good.

Tombaugh was born in Streator, Illinois, in 1906. In 1922, the family moved to Kansas where they established a farm. His plans to attend college were dashed when a hailstorm shredded the family's crops. Perhaps as compensation, he began building telescopes. Unimpressed with commercial equipment, Tombaugh ground his own mirrors and built his own telescopes. He would built more than 30 instruments in his lifetime.

If you know anything about mirrors and lenses, you know temperature can adversely affect them and wind jiggles a telescope. So, using a pick and shovel, Tombaugh dug a pit 24 feet long, eight feet deep, and seven feet wide to house his instruments, shielding them from wind. The pit also maintained a constant temperature. Besides a makeshift observatory, the pit served as the family's root cellar and emergency shelter—Kansas is known to have destructive tornados.

In 1928, using a 23-centimeter reflector he'd built, in part, from a crankshaft salvaged from a 1910 Buick and part of a cream separator, he made detailed observations of Jupiter and Mars. Tombaugh was meticulous in transferring what his eye saw to the paper on which he sketched. This was long before closed-circuit diodes (CCDs) and digital electronics that conveyed images directly from the telescope to a computer monitor. He sent his drawings to Lowell Observatory, hoping for a constructive critique. Instead, he was offered a job. The staff needed an amateur astronomer to operate their astrograph, a photographic telescope, in their search for Planet X.

He was hired in 1929 and took only a year to complete Lowell's search for the elusive planet. Perhaps elusive isn't an appropriate modifier for his discovery; after all, the planet is 4.67 billion miles from earth, orbiting in the Kuiper Belt, and is just two-thirds the diameter of Earth's moon.

With some notoriety, Tombaugh managed to fulfill his goal of attending college, earning a bachelor's degree in astronomy in 1936 and a master's degree in 1939 from the University of Kansas. During summers and following college, he continued working at the observatory.

During his 14 years at the Lowell, Tombaugh carried on searching for astronomical objects. Did he think he'd find something else as exciting as a planet? He discovered hundreds of variable stars and asteroids and two comets. One comet he discovered is called 274P Tombaugh-Tenagra. It orbits the sun in just over nine years. In 1929, he found an asteroid he named after his daughter, Annette. A year later, he added another to his credit and called it Alden, after his son. Others he named 3310 Patsy (1931), 3754 Kathleen (1931), and 3775 Ellenbeth (1931). In 1931, the IAU named one he detected 1604 Tombaugh. While he observed nearly 800 asteroids in his search for Pluto, he is officially credited by the Minor Planet Center with discovering and naming 15.

While engaged in his search for Pluto, he also found many previously unknown star clusters, clusters of galaxies, and a nova. He mapped the Great Perseus-Andromeda stratum of extra-galactic nebulae, one of over 29,000 galaxies he documented.

He left the Lowell Observatory in 1943, in the middle of World War II, to teach navigation to Navy officers at Arizona State College. Following the war, the observatory did not have the financial resources rehire him. Tombaugh became a visiting assistant professor of astronomy at the University of California at Los Angeles until 1946, when he began work at White Sands Missile Range in ballistics research. As chief of optical measurements, he developed tracking telescopes used to photograph rockets and missiles during test flights. Among the instruments he designed is a camera called IGOR — or Intercept Ground Optical Recorder. It remained in use at White Sands for 30 years following its first use in 1951.

From 1953 to 1955, he lead the Near-Earth Satellite Search, an Army project crucial to identifying any small natural satellites in orbit around earth, preparatory to sending rockets and people into space. During this time, he transferred from White Sands to the Physical Science Laboratory of New Mexico State University. In 1959, his research group released the

Near-Earth Satellite Search final report, noting no natural satellites, other than the moon, had been found. NASA could be assured if it launched rockets and later people into space, they were safe from colliding with natural orbiting debris.

From 1958 to 1973, he directed the NMSU photographic Planetary Patrol of Mercury, Venus, Mars, Jupiter, and Saturn. In addition to that project, until 1968, Dr. Tombaugh also conducted research such as studying the geology of Mars and helping choose a location for the Air Force observatory at Sunspot, New Mexico.

By the time he retired in 1973, he and his Planetary Patrol researchers had confirmed the daily rotation period of Mercury, determined the vortex nature of Jupiter's Great Red Spot, and developed a new photographic technique for the small Earth satellite searches. Reflecting on his career late in his life, Tombaugh often said: "I've really had a tour of the heavens."

In August 1992, Robert Staehle, who headed the Pluto Fast Flyby Project at Jet Propulsion Laboratory in La Cañada, California, called Tombaugh and asked if it was all right for him to visit his planet. Tombaugh said, "I told him he was welcome to it, though he's in for one long, cold trip." The call eventually led to the launch of the New Horizons space probe to Pluto in 2006. By then, Clyde Tombaugh had died at age 90 in 1997. A small portion of his cremated remains was placed aboard the spacecraft. The container includes the inscription: "Interned herein are remains of American Clyde W. Tombaugh, discoverer of Pluto and the solar system's 'third zone'"

If Tombaugh's spirit flew with his ashes inside New Horizon to Pluto, he found the planet he discovered is not alone. It it accompanied by five moons we know of: Charon, the mythological ferryman of Hades; Hydra, the nine-headed serpent who battled Heracles; Nix, the Greek goddess of darkness; Styx, the goddess after whom the river in Hades is named; and Kerberos, the dog that guards Pluto's underworld. It's spelled with a K instead of a C to distinguish it from asteroid 1865 Cerberus, which had prior claim to the name.

New Horizons continues to fly away from the sun at a rate of nearly 46,000 feet or nearly nine miles per second. It's headed toward a "cold classical object," a primordial object that had been created when the solar system formed. No one has ever visited an object like this. It could fill in some of the gaps about how our solar system came to be.

The idea of expanding our knowledge of the universe would have pleased Clyde Tombaugh, who is, in a way, making the journey with the spacecraft.

Fred Harvey — Restaurateur
All he wanted was a decent meal

There's lots for travelers to complain about these days. Accommodations don't meet our expectations. Highways are crowded. Security at airports is a pain. And you only get a bag of peanuts flying to your destination.

There's a lot to complain about — but nothing like it was at the end of the 19th century.

In the 30 years after the first transcontinental line was completed in 1869, railroads were rapidly knitting the country together with ribbons of steel. People were on the move — migrants seeking new lives in the West, adventurers exploring a more accessible world, business people expanding into new markets. It was an exciting time, but it had its drawbacks.

Railroads ran on a schedule suitable for trains. They stopped for no more than 20 minutes for water and fuel. That took precedence over customer satisfaction. In fact, jolting along at 20 miles per hour, passengers were only slightly more comfortable — though no less invaluable — than cattle riding in the freight cars. Whatever expectations people from Back East had, they were quickly disillusioned by vast open country, mountains covered in snow well into summer, deserts, and wild prairies.

In most of the small towns of the West, if there were accommodations, they were shoddy. If travelers got hungry, their choice was usually a saloon, where bartenders served greasy, fried meat, mealy beans, rancid bacon, and coffee made fresh once a week. Railroad stations and the towns they served were no place for a genteel man or woman.

To make matters worse, it appears engineers and cafe owners were in cahoots. Within the 20 minute stop, food came too late, or trains left early. The diner had no chance to eat his meal. Untouched meals were often reheated and served hours later to the next round of customers. Railroad men and cafe managers spilt the insidiously achieved rewards.

One man changed all of that because he only wanted a good cup of coffee and a decent meal. He was Fred Harvey, whose name will forever be associated with the Atchison, Topeka and Santa Fe Railroad and the Harvey House restaurants he established all along the line.

Frederick Henry Harvey was born in London in 1835 and emigrated to the United States when he was 15. He worked as a busboy in New York City and, even though he was paid only $2 a day, he kept his eyes open and paid attention, learning the restaurant business.

He left the Big Apple for the Big Easy—although I don't think those names were used in the late 1800s. He intended opening his own restaurant in New Orleans. He never got the chance. What he got was yellow fever.

Instead of New Orleans, Harvey finally got his chance in St. Louis. In 1857, he and a partner started a cafe, which they ran quite profitably. But his partner was sympathetic to the Confederacy. So when the Civil War broke out, he left town, taking with him all the money the two had made.

With a wife and growing family, Harvey had to earn a living. He began working as a mail clerk for the Hannibal and St. Joseph Railroad in 1862 and was so good at his job, he became one of two clerks to sort mail while trains were in transit, becoming part of what came to be called the Railway Mail Service. In time, the Hannibal and St. Joseph was absorbed by the Chicago, Burlington and Quincy Railroad. Harvey continued working for the larger line, eventually—in 1876—being promoted to general western freight agent, based in Leavenworth, Kansas.

A frequent traveler, Harvey was appalled by unsanitary lodging available to him in the West—there were no five-star hotels—and disgusted with poorly prepared food. Having survived yellow fever and other ailments, he knew the risk to his health of both poor lodging and worse food.

Perhaps it was indigestion and concern for bedbugs that finally kindled the idea. Perhaps it was just a bright idea at the right time. With his knowledge of restaurants and his railroad experience, he came to believe he could introduce good food and clean service for his employer's paying customers.

He kept his job at the railroad but opened two cafes with a new partner — one in Wallace, Kansas, and one in Hugo, Colorado. The restaurants did well, even though Harvey had to guide them from a distance. Jeff Rice, Harvey's partner, never shared the high standards Harvey set, and they dissolved the partnership after only a year. Harvey continued operating the cafes but now had devised a system that could link cafes all along the railroad.

His employer, Chicago, Burlington and Quincy Railroad, showed no interest and suggested to try the Atchison, Topeka and Santa Fe. They said the Santa Fe would try anything, like Mikey in that old cereal commercial.

Perhaps not everything, but the Santa Fe liked Harvey's idea. He opened his first Harvey House in Florence, Kansas. The success of Harvey's cafe caused a local newspaper to speculate how long it would be before he lowered his high standards. When he persisted, what he found was a traffic jam at the lunch counter.

Leslie Poling-Kempes, in her book, *The Harvey Girls: Women Who Opened the West,* included this quote of Lucius Beebe: "Travelers positively declined to go further once they had eaten with Fred Harvey. Traffic backed up, and it became necessary for the Santa Fe to open similar houses at other points along its right of way in order that the West might not be settled in just one spot."

In New Mexico, Harvey Houses were operated in Albuquerque, Belen, Carlsbad, Clovis, Deming, Gallup, Lamy, Las Vegas, Raton, Rincon, San Marcial, and Vaughn. They were part of a network that eventually included 86 dining rooms and 15 hotels along the entire length of the Santa Fe railroad.

The system Harvey created was ingenious if nothing else. He knew what passengers wanted was good, hot food at reasonable prices, served so they could eat within the 20-minute scheduled stop. To accomplish this, he devised a series of signals transmitted by engineers, who tooted them on the train's whistle, alerting the cafe staff as the train approached. Porters or conductors took orders and told the engineer how many of each entree needed to be ready upon arrival. This necessitated a limited menu, but that was okay so long as passengers had time to eat.

When the train pulled into the station and customers were seated in the dining room, all they had to ask for was their beverage and what type of pie they wanted.

Harvey hired local cooks but staffed his lunch rooms and dining rooms with young, single women, dressed in iconic uniforms of ankle-length, black and white shirtwaists. They came to be known as Harvey Girls and contributed to the resounding success of Harvey Houses all along the route from Chicago to Los Angeles.

In the 1930s, times were hard. The Great Depression lay heavy on the land, bringing an end — among other things — to the Golden Age of Railroads. Times were also changing. Railroads began including dining cars so people didn't have to rush through a meal while the engine was serviced. And then there was the automobile. People had greater freedom of travel and fewer took the train.

Harvey Houses began closing. They've virtually disappeared in New Mexico. The Harvey House in Gallup is a bus station. In Clovis, Burlington Northern-Santa Fe Railroad uses the Harvey House for storage. In Las Vegas, La Castañeda is currently undergoing renovations by the same owners of La Posada, a fully restored Harvey House in Winslow, Arizona. The iconic El Avarado Hotel in Albuquerque, one of the most striking examples of Mission Revival architecture, was demolished in the 1970s — allegedly without notifying the public who might have wanted to preserve it — to make way for a multimodal transit hub. Only Santa Fe's La Fonda Hotel, once a Harvey House, carries on in the Fred Harvey's tradition.

There's so much more to this story. The decision to use Harvey Girls as hostesses is a critical aspect of Harvey's success. You can read their entire story in Poling-Kempes' book. Harvey Girls came west by the tens of thousands, breaking stifling societal dictates for independence — and perhaps a chance to find a good man to marry. Harvey was instrumental, collaborating with the Santa Fe, in developing the Southwestern Indian Tours, giving railroad travelers a chance to leave the line for three-day auto tours of pueblos, Grand Canyon, and other sites.

And to think, it began just because all Fred Harvey wanted a good cup of coffee and a decent meal.

Hunter Lewis — Missionary Preacher
Families remember the baby caps he crocheted

Episcopalians from Albuquerque, New Mexico, to El Paso, Texas, who were baptized from the early 1900s to the1940s may have a very special memento of the occasion, especially if they were baptized by Reverend Hunter Lewis.

Tucked away in the family chest may be a crocheted cap the circuit preacher made as he walked the roads from village to village throughout the Mesilla Valley of the Rio Grandé.

Born Nicholas Hunter four years after the Civil War, Lewis grew up in Powhatan County, Virginia — about 40 miles west of Richmond. A sickly child that kept him from doing the usual things boys do, he developed two passions — one for God and the other for knitting and crocheting. In1882, he entered Episcopal high school in Alexandria, Virginia, graduating four years later. During that time, he was confirmed in the Emmanuel Episcopal church of Virginia Theological Seminary.

Lewis taught school and tutored students until he was 32 years old, when he entered the Virginia Theological Seminary, from which he graduated in 1904. He accepted a position at the Church of the Holy Communion in Yoakum, Texas. That was a short-lived posting, for a year later he became a missionary in New Mexico, working out of the St. James Episcopal Church in Mesilla Park. For the next 43 years, he traveled the 250-mile-long Mesilla Valley, creating 23 churches or missions.

So what's that have to do with crocheted baby caps? Part may have to do with the fact his wife, Florence Edith Weymouth, died in December 1906, leaving him alone. Without his companion, without his own children, perhaps he compensated. When you check the numbers, you learn, Preacher Lewis—as he was fondly called by people in Mesilla Valley—performed more than 500 weddings, conducted over 500 funerals, and baptized some 1,500 people.

For every baby born into his spiritual care over more than four decades, Preacher Lewis crocheted a baby cap, about 2,500 in total. He also often made booties, sweaters, and blankets, though not for every single child.

Liz Adair, author of the novel, *Counting the Cost*, says her path crossed Preacher Lewis' in Las Palomas, when he baptized her in 1942. "I still have the baptismal cap he gave me on that day," she says, and then adds, the pastor had baptized her mother 25 years earlier.

Preacher Lewis didn't drive. He walked. Although if someone offered a ride, he accepted. In his memoir, *Growing Up in Old Las Cruces*, Leroy Lozier writes, "I would see him walking everywhere. He never put up his thumb to hitchhike."

Lozier continues, "One day I picked him up when I was on my way to go fishing up at Caballo (the reservoir on the Rio Grandé below Elephant Butte dam)." Offered a ride, Lewis climbed in and, once settled in the car, pulled his crocheting out of the black bag he always carried and went to work. It took about three hours to crochet a cap, and the minister worked at his craft whenever time permitted.

Along the way, Lozier says, he asked if they could stop at a saloon in Radium Springs. "I suppose everybody in the community knew him," Lozier writes. So they stopped there, and Lewis went from one end of the bar to the other, holding out his hand. "Everybody would give him 50 cents or a dollar and at that time that was a lot of money," Lozier says. They stopped at a bar in Hatch and a couple others until Lozier reached Caballo. The preacher used the money he collected to minister to anyone in need, Episcopalian or not.

J. Stambaugh tells yet another story featuring the missionary preacher. There were two sisters in Hillsboro who had grown up Southern Baptists but who had never been baptized. Preacher Lewis insisted they get baptized, but the women were "suspicious of being sprinkled." They told Lewis, "They would consent to be baptized only if they could be fully immersed." It was the Dust Bowl years, and there wasn't enough water anywhere in town for them to be submerged.

"Finally, Preacher Lewis scouted a mountain spring that had been dammed," Stambaugh writes. "He was preparing for the service when one of the men who was standing near the sisters pointed out a water snake swimming in the pool. The two sisters decided right then baptism by sprinkling wasn't that bad after all."

Many stories like this one are chocked full of legends and hopeful remembrances. Lewis' story, however, is unembellished fact. As Gandhi is commonly quoted as saying, "The claim I have made is neither extraordinary nor exclusive." He referred to having heard the voice of God before undertaking his 1932 fast. "God rules the lives of all those who surrender themselves without reservation to him."

That's how it is with godly men. That's how it was with Preacher Hunter Lewis. He died in El Paso in 1948.

Allan Houser — Sculptor
Capturing spirits of his ancestors

Allan Houser is perhaps best known as a sculptor, even though he was trained as a painter, and the path he followed to fame was somewhat circuitous.

Though Houser never intended to be known as an Indian artist, his Native American roots went deep. He was, after all, a Chiricahua Apache. You cannot understand his art, nor appreciate his vision, without understanding his past.

Throughout the late 1800s, the Chiricahua living near Ojo Caliente or Warm Springs, just west of Truth-or-Consequences, fought against the U.S. Army and encroaching settlements to retain their ancestral home.

The names of their leaders—Geronimo, Cochise, and Mangas Colo-radas—are legendary. Mangas Coloradas, in fact, was Houser's great grandfather.

When Sam Ha-o-zous, Houser's father, (he later changed his name from his ancestral one) was 14, he and most of the Chiricahua were taken prisoner and shipped in boxcars to Florida. Their imprisonment contin-ued there for some years, when they were moved to Mobile, Alabama, and later to Fort Sill, Oklahoma. After 27 years of imprisonment, the Chiricahua were set free and given an option: return to New Mexico and live with the Mescalero Apache, whom they apparently did not like, or accept a 160-acre parcel of government farmland near Fort Sill.

Sam had married by then and chose to be a farmer. He also became indispensable to Geronimo, serving as his translator.

Allan was born on the farm in 1914, a year after his parents had gained their freedom. He was the first member of his family from the Warm Springs Chiricahua Apache born outside captivity since Geroni-mo's surrender in 1886.

As a youngster, Houser illustrated stories he heard from his par-ents. His father would correct his drawings so they were historically and culturally accurate. To anyone who may have seen the drawings, they would have known he possessed untapped talent.

In his late teens, Houser submitted his drawings to the Santa Fe Indian School. Dorothy Dunn, trained at The Art Institute in Chicago, had established the art program. With a dollar in his pocket, he left Okla-homa in 1932, the year one might say the artist was born.

Dunn trained her students rigorously, developing their skills as painters of what has come to be called "Indian paintings," two-dimen-sional work with flat-color casein and tempera. She encouraged working from personal memory to avoid stylizing Native iconography. Houser became one of her top students but found the program too constricting.

When he struck out on his own in 1939, Houser found the life of an artist hardly bearable. He called it "the first of my starving artist pe-riods." But he earned some commissions and survived. After showing his work at the 1939 New York World's Fair, he received a commission to paint murals at the Department of the Interior's principle building in Washington, D.C. That led to another commission to paint life-size indoor murals for the Department of the Interior. He returned to Fort Sill to study with Olie Nordmark, a muralist from Sweden who encouraged Houser to explore sculpture.

However, World War II intervened, disrupting his career. In the 1940s, now married and with children, Houser moved to Los Angeles to work in construction by day and paint and sculpt by night. He also found time to study European artworks in museums there.

Somehow, somewhere, someone decided Houser *was* a sculptor and commissioned him to create a work for the Haskell Institute in Kansas. The Native American boarding school had lost many graduates to the war and wanted a sculptural memorial to honor them. In 1948, self-taught in sculpture, Houser transformed a four-ton block of Carrara marble, using a jackhammer and hand-made tools, into *Comrades in Mourning,* an iconic work that raised the art world's attention of him.

He won a Guggenheim Fellowship in 1949 and accepted a job teaching at the Intermountain Indian School in Brigham City, Utah. Here Houser taught generations of students the skills, techniques, patience, and tenacity he brought to his own life and work. While at Intermountain, he illustrated seven children's books — including an illustrated biography on the life of his granduncle, Geronimo.

In 1962, Houser joined the faculty of the Institute of American Indian Arts in Santa Fe, where he began to emerge as one of America's most important Native American sculptors. He was 48 years old.

Whether teaching or living in Santa Fe hindered his work, or whether it was the opportunity to join his son and buy the land near Galisteo, Houser *retired* at age 62 to the juniper-dotted hills of southern Santa Fe county. He built a studio and a foundry and began producing an enormous body of work. In the 18 years remaining in his life, he produced more than 80 works in stone, bronze, and steel — a body of work that will define his contributions to art for generations to come.

Houser's son, Philip, spent six years following his father's death in 1994, designing the sculpture garden at the compound, creating settings that best display each of his sculptures. From different vantage points, they are set as individual pieces or subtle groupings, though the groupings never seem contrived, merely coincidental. Even so, observing the juxtaposition of two heroic images of Native Americans at prayer does not diminish the power of either.

Houser's subjects almost exclusively are Native American, mostly Apache and Navajo. They are modernist and, in his later years, abstract. They portray men, women, and children at sacred moments, in prayer or song, celebrating life. They are solemn and serene. They are joyful and mystical. Houser seems to have been able to capture the soul of his subject and incorporate it in the metal or stone.

In *Earth Mother*, for example, you expect the chanting woman embracing her child to turn and sing directly to you, her face is so full of life and energy. In *Prayer Song*, you can feel the power of the man on his knees, his placid face tilted skyward, sensing a revelation that whatever he is praying for will be fulfilled. In the next moment, you imagine he will raise the rattle and feather held in his hands toward heaven. And in *Rendezvous*, Houser has captured the mischievous expression on the face of the young Chiricahua woman, who has slipped away from her chaperone to meet her young man.

Houser did not work from models. His people came from his experience and his imagination. Each piece tells a story. Each captures a moment in time, daring you to enter into the dialog he started and which you now must carry on if you are to know him completely—if you are to know him at all. Even the last piece in the garden is a challenge. It's a four-foot-square by nine-foot-tall block of Carrara marble. Untouched by the artist, it demands you relinquish the reality of what you see and experience the image Houser would have released.

Allan Houser never did a self-portrait, neither painting nor sculpture. But Philip, also an accomplished artist, did a life-size sculpture of his father. It stands near the visitor center in the garden. Houser is wearing a beret at a cocky angle, and Philip captured an expression on his father's face, a sly smile and twinkle in his eye that tells you he knew something of life others are searching for—something you may find in his sculptures if only you study them long enough.

The Hill Family of Shakespeare
Still part of living history

Ghost towns abound in New Mexico. Most are just memories of what they once were; not much more than remnants of an odd building or rounded mounds of melted adobe walls. A few have survived the ravages of time and have been rescued by preservationists. Shakespeare is one such town.

Located a couple miles southwest of Lordsburg, Shakespeare was founded in 1870 when prospectors discovered silver in lodes close enough to the surface for easy mining. Within a short while, the town had 175 buildings and a population of about 3,000.

Then the easy ore gave out. People began leaving. The town was in decline until 1879. The cross-country railroad had been completed by then and a spur built from the main line in Lordsburg. The railroad made it economical to mine lower-grade silver ore, shipping it to a smelter elsewhere. Shakespeare's population stabilized at about 250 people.

During this second silver boom, miners discovered copper, but it was deep and prices in 1885 were too low for economical extraction. By the turn of the century, demand for copper had risen, and miners dug deep—nearly 3,000 feet—to get at the metal. This third boom lasted until 1932.

At the onset of the Great Depression, mining ended at Shakespeare. It seemed the town was destined to expire. That's when Frank and Rita Hill decided to buy the town and surrounding land for $1,250 and make it the headquarters for their ranch. They put a few hundred dollars down and paid ten dollars a month from 1935 until 1950, when they finally got the property free and clear.

The life story of Frank and Rita Hill and their only daughter, Janaloo, is an epic tale repeated time and again across New Mexico. There isn't room here to do more than touch upon it but, if you're a history buff, you'll not want to miss reading *The Hill Family of Shakespeare*, written by Janaloo Hill. It's the story of how a cowboy and a schoolmarm got married and saved a historic ghost town.

What they bought was a collection of derelicts, most in advanced stages of disrepair. There was the Grant House and the Stratford Hotel, a saloon, the mail station and the assay office, the blacksmith, and the general merchandise store.

The general store had the best roof, although it leaked when it rained, which fortunately for desert dwellers isn't often. The back wall had fallen out of the building and been poorly rebuilt. But it had a 30-by-45-foot front room with handsome redwood and pine ceiling. The Hills were able to set up housekeeping there, although the building had neither plumbing nor furnace. The furnace problem was easily solved by installing their Happy Day wood stove. The lack of plumbing required them to carry water daily from a well a quarter mile away and to use an outhouse a hundred feet in the opposite direction. Later, Hill had a well drilled closer to their home and piped the water to a storage tank. Now instead of hauling water a quarter mile, they carried their bucket 30 feet and up a few stairs.

It wasn't the best of living conditions, but they were content to set up their metal frame bed in one side of the large room and their wobbly table and chairs in the other. Orange and apple crates served as cupboards. They had their home, and they were in business.

In time, Janaloo was born on the ranch, and the Hill's lives unfolded. In time, Janaloo grew up and married her own cowboy, Manny Hough, in 1984. Sadly, she died of cancer in 2005. She was 66. Hough is the last of the family to live at Shakespeare.

As Rita Hill assessed the "assets" of their ghost-town ranch, she began to meet people who had lived there earlier and who had returned to show their children their former home. The history of Shakespeare intrigued her, and she collected the stories they told.

There were 15 saloons in Shakespeare. They had names like Police Gazette, Last Chance, and the Silver Dollar. The remaining saloon is representative of the collection. It's a small adobe building with a couple windows, an even smaller bar, and a table and chairs. There are even a few bullet holes in the walls from enthusiastic cowboys.

The Grant House was the Butterfield stage station from 1858 to 1861. Besides its large, welcome fireplace, it's full of cast-iron cookware, tack, and other period artifacts. The front dining room has a large joist supporting the roof and, because trees were scarce in Shakespeare, the joist was used for hangings.

Hough tells the story of two of at least ten men hanged there. Russian Bill apparently cheated investors in a mining claim. Sandy King drank too much, got into too many fights, and was the town troublemaker. When he shot the finger off the clerk at the general store who teased him about buying a silk lace handkerchief, allegedly for a lady friend, he was charged with the crime. Both King and Russian Bill fled on stolen horses only to be caught and brought to justice. However, in Shakespeare, there was no "legal" law; there was just the vigilante committee. Both men were hanged in 1881. Later when a pesky reporter from New York kept pressing for details, the owner of the Grant House informed him Russian Bill was hanged for cheating and horse theft. Sandy King, he said, was hanged because he was a dang nuisance. The reporter asked no more questions.

The Stafford Hotel next door is undergoing restoration. Salvation might be a better name because Hough and the Foundation that operates the town has an ingenious rig slowly pushing a sloping adobe wall back into plum. It'll take time, but time can be had by a building standing since 1858 and hosting notables like Lew Wallace who authored *Ben Hur*, President Rutherford Hayes, and Billy the Kid.

The assay office is perhaps the most completely restored building, its walls stuccoed and a muslin ceiling placed to keep dust from falling on visitors. There are historic glass beakers and vessels along with an ore furnace for sampling ores. There's also a scale enclosed in a box to weigh the most minute quantities of ore without being disrupted by breezes.

There's also a fully functional blacksmith shop, the National Mail and Transport Company, sitting right next to the charred foundation that once held the general merchandise store.

Only fairy tales have truly happy endings. For all the years the Hills lived at Shakespeare, they endured a home without the basic comforts we all take for granted. Then in 1986, the Houghs built an apartment in the basement of the general merchandise building and, because it was below grade, they could finally use gravity to provide indoor water and even a flush toilet. Within a year, a typical New Mexican wind storm caught a loose wire which sparked, smoldered, and set the building on fire. It burned to the ground. They lost not only their home and one of the best of the historic buildings, but also many personal and historic treasures.

Time continues its ravage of ghost towns. Shakespeare is no exception, but those forces harrying the town have met their match, for Manny Hough and the Friends of Shakespeare are persistent preservationists.

Four times a year, Shakespeare Ghost Town hosts a living history event—in April, June, August, and October. Then, Shakespeare comes alive with Union army re-enactors who encamp in town with their tents, historic rifles, and cannon. Watch the blacksmith at work or experience the usual collection of hangings, gunfights, and shady dealings. Based on history, the living history days are not only entertaining but informative.

All that's missing are the Hills—Frank, Rita, and Janaloo—the family that rescued this iconic part of New Mexico history.

Chester Nez—Code Talker
His language—once denied—helped win the war

President George W. Bush draped the ribbon holding the gold medal around the aging Marine's neck, acknowledging his service to his country. Then, instead of shaking the President's hand, the Marine straightened to attention and saluted his commander-in-chief.

The Congressional Gold Medal was one of only 29 awarded, and the recipient was one of the original 29 Navajo Code Talkers. He was Chester Nez.

In his memoir, *Code Talker*, written with Judith Avila, Nez said, "I'm no hero. I just wanted to serve my country."

That country—the United States—had tried its best to deny him his native heritage and culture. The Bureau of Indian Affairs (BIA) decided

he and other Navajo children should go to boarding school to be accul-
turated into mainstream American life. He was not allowed to speak his
birth language—the very Diné language that led to the famous code. His
Navajo clothing was confiscated, and he was forced to wear blue cover-
alls—"white man's" clothing. His shoulder length hair was cut so short,
he felt his scull had been shaved. He suffered deprivation, bullying, and
discrimination. When he finally enlisted in the Marines, he could not
vote—a privilege extended to Native Americans only in 1948.

You might ask yourself, "Why would a man risk his life in a war
involving a country that had denied him basic rights afforded to all citizens?" The answer to the question is the story of Chester Nez.

Nez' family will tell you they don't really know when he was born.
He remembers a situation in which he said he was living in his sixth
spring. Traditional Navajo don't use a calendar like the average American does. Presumably, when he was enrolled in the BIA's boarding
school, his birth date was fixed at January 23, 1921.

Nez' mother died some years before his sixth spring, and he said he
didn't remember her. Again, in traditional Navajo culture, children are
not allowed around terminally ill relatives. And when his mother died,
he was not allowed to attend the funeral. Woman prepared her body for
burial. Her father took her to the gravesite, a place of which he never
informed anyone. There is fear among Navajo, that unsettled spirits can
"infect" a living person with the *chindi*—ghost sickness. They avoid the
dying and vacate hogans in which they die, never to return. They also
never again mention the deceased person's name.

He lived with his aunt and grandmother in the Checkerboard
Area—land outside the Navajo Nation divided into allotments for
Navajo, with other parcels owned by Anglos and Hispanics. It was hard
enough to live on the reservation. It was even harder living in the Checkerboard. Nez said, "We could go for three or four days without eating."

Lack of food wasn't the only hardship. The house he grew up in
did not have electricity until 2008, and clean water had to be carried some
distance from the well to the house.

The family herded sheep and goats, at one time owning more
than 300 head. Chester, called *Betoli* [his Navajo name] by his relatives,

traveled with the herd as it was moved from grazing area to area. They had a single "sheep" horse, used to haul possessions, a white, 80-pound sheepdog, the family called Snow, and several other dogs to herd and guard animals from coyotes. During summer, they slept in the open under blankets, cooked on pit fires, and carried their water in a large, skin bag. The animals were easy to care for. The Navajo love for their land and animals was translated into companionable relations between people and livestock.

Each morning, Nez would slip his shirt, in which he slept, into his shorts. He said they were a "hodgepodge of patches and mends." His feet had hard calluses because he preferred going barefoot when weather permitted. In reality, his family had little ready cash to keep him in shoes.

Life may have been hard but it was what the Diné knew, so it didn't seen burdensome.

When the BIA informed Nez' father the boy was to attend school, the family discussed his education. The discussion was necessary because Navajo families are matrilineal — based on the women's kinship. The final decision was Nez' grandmother's. He said he liked the idea of learning to read and write. He thought, someday he might have to work off the reservation and knowledge gained in school could be useful. His grandmother said, "Good. It's settled then."

It was not easy to live with. Nez said at school he was always hungry. "I was never able to eat what I wanted, when I wanted, or as much as I wanted." His breakfast at home consisted of blue-corn mush and goat's milk. Midday meals were tortillas and goat's cheese. Occasionally, they had meat. In his memoir, Nez relates hunting a porcupine with his older brother. They thought porcupine, baked in a dirt oven, was a delicacy.

At school, children were forbidden to speak Diné. They had to speak English, even when they knew none of the language, or be punished. It took some time for him to get used to responding to Chester, rather than *Betoli*. When Nez tried to help a younger boy button his jumpsuit, teaching him how in Diné, his teacher shouted, "English only," and slapped him across the face with the back of her hand.

How he survived is a testament to his desire to improve himself. That became vitally important in 1935, when the BIA determined the Navajo had too many sheep and goats, which were, in their words, destroying the land through overgrazing. On his grandmother's land, the BIA brought a bulldozer and dug a trench. Then they killed 300 of the family's herd—never giving consideration the Navajo measured wealth by their sheep and goats. Now there was no wool, no milk, and no meat to sustain them economically.

Five months after Pearl Harbor was attacked, Nez, now 21 years old, enlisted in the Marines. The military had asked them to. They had something in mind but did not inform the Navajo men who joined up. After basic training, Nez and 28 others—he claims there were three additional men, bringing the total to 32—were assigned to the 382nd Platoon and told to devise a code in their Diné language. What was once denied them now became a critical element in military communications.

Code Talkers were not new to the military. They had been used during World War I. Cherokee code talkers of the 30th Infantry Division served alongside the British during the Second Battle of the Somme. Choctaw men in the 36th Infantry Division used their language to communicate within the American Expeditionary Forces during key battles in the Meuse-Argonne offensive in France.

Hitler knew about the World War I code talkers' success and sent linguists posing as tourists and scholars to the U.S. to learn Native American languages before the outbreak of World War II. Mastering the gender of German nouns, each of which requires a *der, die,* or *das* article, proved far easier for linguists than learning complex Native American languages and their various dialects.

So it is probably no surprise, the Allies employed Comanche code talkers during the invasion of Normandy and in the signal company of the 4th Infantry Division as it moved across Europe. Twenty-seven Meskwaki men, members of the Sac and Fox tribes, used their language against the Germans in the conquest of North Africa.

It seems a shame these people have been overshadowed by the Navajo Code Talkers. Perhaps the reason is the number of Navajo who fought in the Pacific—more than 450—or perhaps the ferocity of island-hopping battles and the unyielding resolve of the Japanese to relinquish territory. Whatever the reason, the Navajo stand out among Native Americans who communicated critical battle information during the war.

Nez and his fellow Marines crafted their code, assigning a word to each letter of the alphabet and using several hundred other words to indicate specific ranks, countries, and materiel. For example, a dive bomber was called *gini* — chicken hawk. A submarine was called *besh-lo* — iron fish. And a general was called *Bih-keh-he* — war chief. When words didn't appear to fit a rank, they used different names, calling a caption *Besh-le-gai-nah-kin*, for his two silver bars.

The Code Talkers attended one landing after another. Their role was communications, but they often had to fight for survival and occasionally died on islands for which their people at Dinétah — the Navajo homeland — not only had no words but no concept of where their men had fought and died.

So, why fight for a country that had denied him his basic rights?

In his memoir, Nez relates a conversation he had with Roy Begay, a friend who would be by his side for life. When Begay asked what he thought, he said, "Our country has joined the war. I think the military will want us. We are warriors."

Like other Native Americans, the Navajo had been born to a warrior tradition. And like other Navajos, Nez wrote, "We saw ourselves as inseparable from the earth we lived upon. As protectors of what is sacred, we were eager to defend our land."

And so Nez rose above the hardships and the prejudice, insults, bullying, and taunts he had experienced as a youth, and he fought for the country that was his as much as any Harvard brahmin or Texas cowboy.

In 2014, Chester Nez died at age 93. He was the last of the original 29 Navajo Code Talkers.

Ralph Hanks—War Hero
He held four aces in his hand

In Christmas Tree Canyon, a few miles north of Mora along New Mexico Highway 434, is a log cabin. On seeing it, if you are reminded of Daniel Boone in the Kentucky wilderness, you wouldn't be far wrong.

Until 2014, this was the home of Ralph Hanks, Captain U.S. Navy (retired). Like Boone, he was an adventurer and, like Tennessee's Davy Crocket a bit later, he was also a warrior and hero.

Like many of Hanks' generation, this story begins the year before Japan's sneak attack on Pearl Harbor in December 1941.

Hanks had wanted to become a Naval aviator but could not pass the physical. Even though he was training in a civilian pilot flight course, while in college, he was found to be color blind.

"A friend told me I could squint and pass the test," Hanks says. "I did that, and the numbers just popped right out."

But he was also underweight and had a slight heart murmur the Navy didn't like.

"The Navy gave physicals every month," he says. "And every month I would fail it." Finally, he gave up on the Navy and tried to enlist in the Canadian Air Force. "They seemed to be taking anyone with a warm body."

Hanks continues, "By that time I had a couple hundred hours in flight time, so they gave me a railroad ticket to Hollywood to take their flight test. I passed their test, and they said they would call me."

The next morning, Hanks decided to try the Navy one more time before joining up with the Canadians. "I passed their physical with no strain," he says, "so I plum forgot about the Canadian Air Force. I had my ticket to join the Navy."

His enlistment date was October 30, 1941. "I'd only been in the Navy a few weeks when the Japanese hit Pearl Harbor," he says. "We thought their next target was going to be the West Coast. The night they hit Pearl Harbor, I was parading up and down the roof of a hanger in the

Oakland Naval Reserve Air Base, expecting the Japanese to arrive any moment. They never did, of course."

Hanks' training began in earnest. He endured six weeks of elimination training in Oakland, where the Navy tried to disqualify anyone who had problems flying. Next, he spent nine months in Pensacola, Florida.

"That was pretty easy," Hanks explains, "because I'd had a couple hundred hours of flight time, and most people there had no flight time. The Navy finally woke up to the fact fifteen of us had previous flight training, so they gave us the afternoons off at the beach. The beach grew old after three days."

He and the other cadets decided to find out what was going on at the outlying airfields. Planes were assigned to instructors and students who'd signed up for them.

"We decided to put our name of the board to see what happened. We'd go out as an instructor and pilot. For about six weeks, we were getting a free ride every morning. We just had a ball for about a hundred hours of flight time."

From Pensacola, Hanks began gunnery training in SNJs at an airfield west of Miami. The SNJ was the Navy's version of the famous North American AT-6 Texas trainer.

Hanks' adventure turned serious on one flight. The engine of his plane quit, and he attempted to land on the Tamiami Trail, but trees were so close to the highway he knew he would hook a wing if he tried. So he cranked up his wheels and bellied into the swamp alongside the road.

"I forgot to close the ventilators on my airplane," he says. Ventilators along the leading edge of the wing forced air into the cockpit. "I set that airplane in three-feet of water and, instead of air coming out of those ventilators, two solid streams of water hit me right in the chest. But I made a good landing. That was my first crash landing."

If you know your World War II history, you know the aircraft carrier Lexington was sunk during the Battle of the Coral Sea in May 1942. A carrier under construction in Boston was then named Lexington. She was launched in September 1942 and commissioned in February 1943. Hanks was assigned to the VF-16 fighter squadron and sailed to Pearl Harbor. He arrived on August 8, 1943. He was finally in the war.

Hanks' squadron of F6F Hellcat fighters were initially used in an unusual way. The Lexington would sail southwest of Pearl Harbor on Monday, bomb military targets and crater runways on Japanese-held islands, and return to port by Friday.

"We spent our weekends in Honolulu on Waikiki Beach," Hanks said.

That was his first introduction to war. The Navy was attacking Tarawa. "We were the first ones to hit Tarawa. We hit it every week until there was hardly a palm tree standing on that island."

Then the Marines landed. Hanks says, "We lost about three thousand Marines. They had to wade in about a mile through three feet of water. Japanese mowed them down as they came in."

During the November 1943 Battle of Tarawa, the Lexington sent its air group to engage Japanese aircraft heading toward the island. One of the pilots spotted the planes and radioed, "Many bogies, ten o'clock down." There were about 20 Japanese planes approaching, and the wing commander finally gave the order to attack.

"Go get'em Airdales," the commander said. The squadron was known as the Pistol Packin' Airdales. Hanks was the first one to engage the enemy aircraft.

"They hadn't seen us before we hit them," he says. In five minutes, in his first air-to-air combat, Hanks shot down five Japanese aircraft. Three were Mitsubishi "Zeros" and two were Mitsubishi "Hamp" dive bombers.

"I splashed five," he reports. "I saw two more that seemed to be leaving the fight and dove toward them. I was coming up on their tail ready to shoot them both down. I pulled the trigger. All I got was three pops. I was out of ammunition. So I wheeled back 180 degrees. I had so much speed I ran off to leave them. I headed back to the ship and was the first to return from the skirmish."

That day, the Hellcats of the Lexington downed 17 of the 20 Japanese aircraft, and Hanks qualified as an ace.

By June 1944, the Navy knew the Japanese fleet was in the Pacific but was having trouble finding it. Then word came, it was in a certain quadrant on the sea charts. Twelve pilots, including Hanks, volunteered to reconnoiter the area. It was a dangerous mission. Far from the carrier, the pilots knew they could run out of fuel. And, if they found the Japanese, they would be twelve against a hornet's nest. They flew 300 miles out to and across the quadrant, near the operational range of their airplanes, then headed back.

"We were all low on fuel," Hanks says. "I had about six hundred pounds when we sighted the ship." Others had less fuel and landed ahead of him. "I got aboard with just enough fuel to land."

While the 12 volunteers were exploring their quadrant, another plane spotted the Japanese fleet in the opposite direction. All airplanes in the task force were committed to the fight. The volunteers got back too late to be serviced and sent out.

"We had to watch what one of the commanders called the Marianas Turkey Shoot," Hanks says. The name stuck, and the Battle of the Philippine Sea is known by it to this day. "A lot of guys got shot down on that trip. Many more ran out of fuel and went into the water."

Hanks continues, "After that, we flew combat air patrols between Guam and Saipan. It was on one of these patrols I got my sixth airplane. I saw this plane coming down. I caught up with him, went in, and with one burst burned him."

At Eniwetok, Hanks' air group was ordered back to San Diego. It had served its time and was replaced.

Following the war, Hanks spent three years testing jet planes at the Patuxent Naval Air Test Center in Maryland. He flew the FJ-3—the Navy's version of the F-86 Sabre jet—as well as the FH-1 Phantom. While testing the Phantom, he again encountered problems that resulted in a crash landing. But any pilot will tell you, any landing you walk away from is a good landing.

Hanks time as a test pilot gave him more jet time than most other pilots. And that's what got him into the Blue Angels. He explains he requested and was assigned to the Navy's first jet squadron.

"I got a pretty good reputation as a jet pilot because I had more time in jets than all those other new guys put together. They were just learning how to fly jets. I was naturally trying to make the best impression I could. Our operations officer was Johnny Magda."

It turns out Magda was tapped to form the Blue Angels. During an air show, one of the pilots crashed and died. Magna asked Hanks if he would be interested in joining his team. "When I got this chance to come to the Blue Angels I said it was a no-brainer. When do you want me?"

Hanks complains he didn't get any practice flights with the team, principally because Magda said he had more jet flight time than the entire Blue Angel squadron combined. He was finally accepted when he bet the team he could do a slow roll on take off, something pilots said was impossible.

That was a misnomer, as Hanks explains. "It's really not on take off. You have to get 300 knots to make a slow roll that close to the ground." He was flying a propeller-driven F8F Bearcat. "That F-8F would take off in about 400 feet. I just took it a few inches off the ground, took the wheels up, and got to the end of the runway. By that time, I had 300 knots, and I could do a slow roll if I was careful. You've got to be sure to get the nose well above the horizon if you're going to do a slow roll at that low altitude. When you get an airplane's wings vertical, there's no lift. You roll the first 90 degrees, you get vertical, and the airplane's going to fall. You hit vertical again when you tuck the other wing under. It's pretty hairy. You've got to be a damn good pilot to do it."

Still, he wasn't getting the flight time he wanted. "John wasn't paying attention to me. The squadron was going to war," Hanks says, referring to the conflict in Korea. "I was happy to get a chance to shoot down some more airplanes so I went to California with them." In California, he was told he was not eligible for sea duty and was sent to Whiting Field in Florida.

Now, when you think about Top Gun, you think Miramar Naval Air Station near San Diego and Tom Cruise flying F-14 Tomcat fighters. However, the Navy's first jet training unit was in Florida, and Hanks was the flight officer — the first commander of Top Gun.

That was a low point in Hanks' career. He was not only a flier who was on the ground teaching others to fly, but he also lost a good friend. During combat in Korea, John Magda was hit by an antiaircraft shell, leaving the rear of his plane on fire. He was told to eject but chose instead to make a sea landing. The plane burst into a ball of fire and, Hanks says, "That was the last anybody ever saw of him."

That brings us to Christmas Tree Canyon in New Mexico. Hanks was involved in testing reconnaissance equipment for the Navy. He flew his jet back and forth across north central New Mexico, discovering the state wasn't all high plains and desert. "You have some high mountains here," he says, "like the kind in California where I grew up."

He and his wife, Frances, found a real-estate agent who showed them Christmas Tree Canyon. "We found three places about this size...1800 acres. They were all about $30 to $35 an acre. I up and bought this right away for $10,000 down and the rest on a 17-year loan at $225 a month." Now as a developer, Hanks subdivided his land and sold six lots the first day. "That paid off the loan," he says. "This whole place has not cost me a penny."

Instead of flying airplanes, Hanks turned to "flying" a bulldozer. "You still fly with both hands and both feet," he says, "except you can cover up your mistakes."

They cleared out a pasture and used the harvested logs to build their home. They used rocks on the property for the foundation. Then, Hanks — who found an interest and talent in woodworking — built all their living room, dining room, and bedroom furniture — as well as cabins for six other families in the canyon.

There's probably more to this story, but Ralph's mule began to hee-haw for him, and he had to go tend to his four-legged friend.

After 40 years in Christmas Tree Canyon, Ralph Hanks died on March 13, 2014. He was 95 years old. Frances, his wife of 58 years, had preceded him in 2002.

John Stapp — Aerospace Medical Researcher
Fastest man on earth

Who is the fastest man on earth? Some would say Jamaican Olympian Usaine Bolt, who sprints at 27 miles per hour. Others think it's George Poteet, who drove his *Speed Demon* across the Bonneville salt flats at 439 miles per hour.

But there is another man to whom the title belongs. He wasn't an athlete. Nor was he a thrill-seeker. And he no longer holds the title, but he was the first. The man is Dr. John Paul Stapp, a colonel in the Air Force. He was a medical researcher, who rode a rocket-powered sled across New Mexico's Tularosa Basin faster than a .45-calibre bullet.

Why on earth would a man subject himself to such extremes? It wasn't fame or fortune that propelled him. It was knowledge. Stapp said, "I have a missionary spirit. When asked to do something, I do it. I took my risks for information that will always be of benefit. Risks like that are worthwhile."

Born to Baptist missionary parents in Salvador de Bahia, Brazil, Stapp entered the Army Air Corps in October 1944 as a medical doctor. Assigned to the Aero Medical Laboratory at Wright Field in Dayton, Ohio, he climbed aboard a stripped-down B-17 bomber not much more than fuselage and engines. While it cruised at altitudes above 40,000 feet, Stapp tested oxygen systems in the unpressurized, freezing aircraft, using himself as a guinea pig. He was attempting to answer questions critical to the future of aviation. Could men survive at extremely high altitudes? Could they keep from freezing, becoming severely dehydrated, or incapacitated by decompression sickness — known as "the bends"? Stapp tackled the problems one-by-one and resolved them. The riddle of the bends seemed insurmountable. However, he found the answer after nearly 65 hours in the air. He discovered, if a pilot breathed pure oxygen for 30 minutes prior to takeoff, symptoms could be avoided entirely. It was an enormous breakthrough, and it changed Dr. Stapp's life forever.

Though he had figured on practicing pediatrics once World War II had ended, Stapp found aerospace medical research so fulfilling he made it his career.

In 1947, Stapp accepted an assignment to the deceleration project. The idea behind the project was how to design airplanes in which pilots could survive crashes. At the time, experts believed the maximum force the human body could survive was 18 G's — or 18 times the force of gravity during which a 175-pound man experiences momentary forces of more than 3,000 pounds.

At Muroc Air Force Base — later renamed Edwards AFB — in the Mojave Desert, the Air Force was constructing a track down which a rocket-sled would be propelled. At one end, engineers installed hydraulic brakes that would slow the sled from 150 mph to 75 mph in a fifth of a second. When it did, G forces would be produced equivalent to those experienced in an airplane crash.

The 15-foot-long sled, called *Gee Whiz*, was comprised of welded tubes and sat on a series of magnesium slippers. On top was a metal cab that accommodated the test subject seated forward, backward, or lying prone.

The initial occupant of the sled was a 185-pound dummy named Oscar Eightball. All tests were expected to be run with dummies, but Stapp had other ideas. Northrup Project Manager George Nichols explained, when Stapp saw Oscar Eightball, he walked over and patted it. "We're not going to use these. You can throw this away." Nichols quoted Stapp. "I'm going to be the test subject."

It took some time to get the bugs worked out of the sled. Brakes failed time and again. On one test run, the brakes locked up at high speed. True to Newton's Second Law of Motion, Oscar obediently sailed on, right through a wooden windscreen. He left his rubber face behind in the wood and soared another 700 feet downrange.

Thirty-five test runs later, Stapp felt engineers had obtained sufficient experience to attempt a manned run. Ever the cautious scientist, on the first ride Stapp used only one rocket. He faced backwards to minimize the acceleration effects and G-load. The sled barely reached 90 mph, and the deceleration was only about 10 Gs. The next day, Stapp added two more rockets. The sled accelerated to 200 mph, but the doctor was hardly affected by the ride. The secrets of human deceleration seemed well within his reach.

By August 1948, Stapp had completed 16 runs, surviving not just 18 G's but 35, yet he felt he was still far from the limit. Initially, he refused to let anyone else ride the sled, fearing if test pilots, who were notorious "hog-doggers," rode, they would skew the data. He endured bruises where harness straps dug into his shoulders and other minor injuries. Most disturbingly, though, he suffered blurry vision. Blood left his eyeballs and pooled towards the back of his head, resulting in a "white out." During later tests, when he faced forwards and the blood was pushed up against his retinas, Stapp would experience "red outs" caused by broken capillaries and hemorrhaging. When it came to G forces, he learned eyes were the most vulnerable part of human anatomy.

Stapp's research on the decelerator had profound implications for both civilian and military aviation. Facing backwards in an aircraft seat was the safest for passengers and required little harness support. Commercial airlines were made aware of these findings but still use forward-facing seats. His work also showed a pilot could walk away from crashes when properly protected by harnesses if the seat didn't break loose. Further, the triangular-shaped harness Stapp developed was superior to old lap belts. His concept was adopted in 1959 by Volvo designer Nils Bohlin and introduced in automobiles as standard equipment. A simple lap belt is all you'll find on every commercial airliner in use today.

Stapp was eventually transferred to Holloman Air Force Base, near Alamogordo, New Mexico, where he got an even faster sled, named *Sonic Wind*. It was on this sled in June 1956, he became the fastest man on earth. Sitting in the forward position, he shot down the track, reaching a speed of 632 mph, breaking the land speed record. (It was never officially recognized by the Fédération Internationale de l'Automobile, which sanctions records.) The sled then decelerated to a dead stop in 1.4 seconds, producing pressures 46.2 times the pull of gravity. In that eye-blink of time, Colonel Stapp's normal 175 pound weight would have felt like 8,085 pounds.

When asked how it felt, Stapp said, "It's like being assaulted in the rear by a fast freight train." When questioned about what he was thinking during the countdown, he said, "Paul, it's been a good life."

Following his record-breaking ride, Stapp experienced loss of sight but, it turned out, he was blind only a few hours. He did achieve a raccoon look with two black eyes brought on because his eyeballs had shot forward in their sockets.

On his 29 rocket-sled rides, Stapp suffered broken ribs, eye hemorrhages, concussion, loss of dental fillings, abdominal hernia, fractured coccyx, and, even once, a broken wrist. He was prepared to continue his experiments riding the *Sonic Wind* to speeds of 1,000 mph. But, because of concerns for his health, the Air Force grounded him after his fastest ride.

Known for his sharp wit, Stapp inspired Murphy's Law in 1949 when he suffered a failure during one of his rides. Captain Edward A. Murphy was an assistant who had designed a harness with sensors measuring G forces. There were exactly two ways each of the 16 sensors could be installed. Murphy put each one in the wrong way. As Stapp climbed off the sled, his eyes bloodshot and harness-strap sores bleeding, the sensors registered zero. The run had been useless.

Murphy was heard to say, "If there are two or more ways to do something and one of those results in a catastrophe, then someone will do it that way." An inveterate collector of aphorisms, Stapp published his logbook, in which he had popularized an edited-version of Murphy's Law: *Anything that can go wrong will go wrong.*

Stapp was inducted into the International Space Hall of Fame at the New Mexico Museum of Space History in 1979 and into the National Aviation Hall of Fame in 1985. He also was recipient of the Air Force Cheney Award for Valor and the Lovelace Award from NASA for aerospace medical research.

When asked if there were any lasting side effects from his dangerous experiments, Stapp said, "All the lunches and dinners I have to go to now."

Colonel Dr. John Paul Stapp died at his home in Alamogordo on November 13, 1999. He was 89 years old.

Bibliography

Chamberlain, Kathleen P. *In the Shadow of Billy the Kid: Susan McSween and the Lincoln County War*. Albuquerque, New Mexico: University of New Mexico Press, 2013.

Cleaveland, Agnes Morley. *No Life For A Lady*. Lincoln, Nebraska: University of Nebraska Press, 1977.

Crichton, Kyle Samuel. *Law and Order, Ltd: The Rousing Life of Elfego Baca of New Mexico*. Santa Fe, New Mexico: Sunstone Press, 2014.

Evans, Max. *Long John Dunn of Taos, From Texas Outlaw to New Mexico Hero*. Santa Fe, New Mexico: Clear Light Publishers, 1952.

Hill, Janaloo. *The Hill Family of Shakespeare*. Shakespeare, New Mexico: Janaloo Hill, 2001.

Jeffries, Eric Scott. "The Historic Committee Presents, Hannett's Joke: Route 66," Santa Fe, New Mexico: *New Mexico Bar Journal*, 2000.

Kessell, John. *Kiva, Crown and Cross*. Albuquerque, New Mexico: University of New Mexico Press, 1987.

Lacy, Ann and Valley-Fox, Anne. *Outlaws and Desperados*. Santa Fe, New Mexico: Sunstone Press, 2008.

Levine, Frances. *Doña Teresa Confronts the Spanish Inquisition: A Seventeenth-Century New Mexican Drama*. Norman, Oklahoma: University of Oklahoma Press, 2016.

Lozier, Leroy. *Growing Up in Old Las Cruces*. Las Cruces, New Mexico: Leroy Lozier, 2012.

Magoffin, Susan. *Down the Santa Fe Trail and into Mexico: The Diary of Susan Shelby Magoffin, 1846–1846* Lincoln, Nebraska: University of Nebraska Press, 1982.

McDonald, Julie. *Unbreakable Dolls: True Stories of Amazing Pioneer Women.* Julie McDonald, 2012.

Myers, Joan. *Pie Town Woman.* Albuquerque, New Mexico: University of New Mexico Press, 2001.

Nez, Chester with Avila, Judith. *Code Talker: The First and Only Memoir by One of the Original Navajo Code Talkers of WW II.* New York, New York: Berkley Publishing Group, 2011.

Poling-Kempes, Lesley. *The Harvey Girls: Women Who Opened the West.* Cambridge, Massachusetts: De Capo Press, 1989.

Rickards, Colin. *Sheriff Pat Garrett's Last Days.* Santa Fe, New Mexico: Sunstone Press, 2007.

Sager, Stan. *Viva Elfego: The Case for Elfego Baca, Hispanic Hero.* Santa Fe, New Mexico: Sunstone Press, 2008.

Sides, Hampton. *Blood and Thunder: The Epic Story of Kit Carson and the Conquest of America.* New York, New York: Anchor Books, 2006.

Ann, Stalcup. *America's Secret Weapon: Navajo Code Talkers of World War II.* Santa Fe, New Mexico: Sunstone Press, 2017.

Stanley, F. *Desperados of New Mexico.* Santa Fe, New Mexico: Sunstone Press, 2015.

— — —. *No Tears for Black Jack Ketchum.* Santa Fe, New Mexico: Sunstone Press, 2008.

Stuart, David E. *Anasazi America.* Albuquerque, New Mexico: University of New Mexico Press, 2000.

Thomas, Diane H. *The Southwestern Indian Detours: The Story of the Fred Harvey/ Santa Fe Railway Experiment in 'Detourism.'* Phoenix, Arizona: Hunter Publishing Co., 1978.

Yurth, Cindy. "Barboncito and Standoff at Fortress Rock." *Navajo Times.* June 4, 2009.

Readers Guide

1. Sally Rooke and Black Jack Ketchum are obviously hero and villain respectively. Which personality traits and behavioral characteristics define a hero and a villain? Why do you think Sally is one and Black Jack the other? Explain and defend your choice.

2. Modesty is a significant personality trait among some people. It often shrouds heroism. After reading the stories about Ralph Hanks, Clyde Tombaugh, and John Stapp, how would you classify their acts? Would you consider them heroes? If so, why?

3. Sometimes curiosity and subsequent acts of bravery can be disguised as heroism. How would you classify the adventure of James Larkin White? Why do you think he was a hero? Why a daring adventurer? What distinguishes the two?

4. New Mexico Governor Arthur Hannett was a politician. Like most politicians, he didn't always follow "the rules." Was his act to carve a road between Santa Clara and Albuquerque in 1927 one of villainy? If so, why do you believe that?

5. How would you classify the acts of Bernardo Gruber, *El Alémán*? How about Diego Romero, Captain of the Apache Nation? These are very different stories. Are they about heroes or villains? Why do you think they are either hero or villain?

6. There is yet another human characteristic present in this collection of stories: that of the tragic victim. Their lives may start out as heroic or even villainous but the outcome ends as neither. How would you characterize Doña Teresa, wife of the New Mexican governor during the Spanish Colonial period, and Juan Maria Agostini-Justiniani, the hermit of La Cueva? Hero, villain, or victim? Explain your choice.

7. Some people go about their lives, doing what they think is best. The outcome of their actions perhaps can make them heroes. Fabián Garcia and Sadie Orchard are examples of two very different people. What about their lives would lead you to consider them heroes?

8. Why would you consider Edward Beale a hero, when the heart of this story is about blazing a wagon road across the Southwest with a herd of camels? What about his life would lead you to that conclusion?

9. Maria Gertrudis Barceló and Chester Nez could both be considered heroes. If you agree, what about their lives leads you to mark them as such?

10. Sheriff Pat Garrett's life is full of heroic and villainous acts. He befriended Billy the Kid, then shot him dead. He served as sheriff trying to solve the murder of Albert Fountain and his eight-year-old son, Henry, but failed to get re-elected from drunkenness. He died under mysterious circumstances. Would you consider him a hero or a villain? Why?

11. John Dunn and Roy Bean are to colorful characters whose lives paint the Southwest. How would you characterize their lives: hero or villain? Explain your choice.

12. Elfego Baca could be considered daring or careless. He could be considered a staunch supporter of the rule of law or arrogant. But was he a hero or a villain? What about his life and this story leads you to your choice?

13. The acts of heroes are sometimes just considered bravery. Other times their actions could make them seem as saviors. How would you define the acts of Kit Carson in the story about Ann White and Chief Barboncito at Fortress Rock?

14. Albert Pfeiffer's life in the West, fighting Ute, Apache, and Navajo warriors, is the stuff movies are made of. You could imagine John Wayne in the role. But, is Pfeiffer a hero or a villain? What makes you think he is either...or both?

15. Heroism is not always accompanied by heroic acts. Sometimes it's simply a matter of survival. Would you consider the story of Cathay Williams one of heroism or survival? Why?

16. What, in your opinion, makes Fred Harvey and Allan Houser heroes? Are they actually heroes or just very successful men at what they did? Justify your choice.

www.ingramcontent.com/pod-product-compliance
Lightning Source LLC
Chambersburg PA
CBHW022009080426
42733CB00007B/536